P9-CCQ-628

THE ONLY GAMING ANNUAL YOU NEED!

2019 GAME ON!

EDITOR IN CHIEF
Jon White

EDITOR
Dan Peel

CONTRIBUTORS
Stephen Ashby, Louise Blain, Wesley Copeland, Aiden Dalby, Zoe Delahunty-Light, Jon Denton, Ian Dransfield, Fraser Gilbert, Ross Hamilton, Darran Jones, Luke Kemp, Carrie Mok, Drew Sleep, Paul Walker-Emig, Mitch Wallace, Alan Wen, Josh West

LEAD DESIGNER
Adam Markiewicz

DESIGNERS
Lora Barnes, Steve Dacombe, Andy Downes, Claire Evison, Ali Innes, Will Shum, Jordan Travers, Perry Wardell-Wicks, Kimberly Winters

PRODUCTION
Sarah Bankes, Amy Best, Philippa Grafton, Ross Hamilton, Russell Lewin, April Madden, Nikole Robinson

PHOTO CREDITS
Paul Hackett (p.132)

COVER IMAGES
Street Fighter V ©CAPCOM U.S.A., INC.
"Crash Bandicoot ™&© 2018 Activision Publishing Inc."
Super Mario Odyssey © Nintendo 2018
Halo © Microsoft 2018
Sea of Thieves © Rare 2018
Minecraft © Mojang 2018
Overwatch © Blizzard Entertainment, Inc 2018
Stardew Valley © ConcernedApe 2018

STARDEW VALLEY

Build, explore, make friends, and more in this gorgeous farm sim RPG. There's so much to see and do, and hours of fun to be had.

Games can be amazing, but it's important that you know how to stay safe, especially when playing online. These ten simple tips will help you to have fun while playing. Follow these and you can have a great time, while your parents can rest easy in the knowledge that you know how to stay safe.

1. Discuss and agree on rules with your parents regarding how long you can stay online, what websites you can visit on the internet, and what apps and games you can use.
2. Remember to take frequent breaks during gaming sessions.
3. Never give out personal information such as passwords, your real name, phone number, or anything about your parents.
4. Never agree to meet in person with someone you've met online.
5. Tell your parents or a teacher if you come across anything online that makes you feel uncomfortable, upset, or scared.
6. Whenever you're online, be nice to other people and players. Never say or do anything that might hurt someone else's feelings or make them feel unhappy.
7. Pay attention to age ratings on games. They exist for a reason—to help protect you from any inappropriate content, not to stop you having fun!
8. Don't download or install software or apps to any device, or fill out any forms on the internet, without checking with the person that owns the device you're using first.
9. If you play mobile games outside, be aware of your surroundings at all times, and don't play alone—always have a friend or family member with you.
10. When using streaming services, always check with an adult before changing to a different video or game.

CONTENTS

CONTENTS

WHAT A YEAR!

And **what a time to be a gamer!** We've seen the return of Mario and Link, witnessed the arrival of the most powerful console the world has ever seen, and played hundreds of brilliant new games. And that's not all! There's so much more to look forward to.

The Nintendo Switch continued to blow us away, with *Super Mario Odyssey* and Nintendo Labo among the highlights of an incredible roster. We finally got our hands on the Xbox One X, Microsoft's challenger to the PS4 Pro and the most powerful console on the planet. With it came a host of awesome experiences and exclusives, including the likes of *Sea of Thieves*, *Cuphead*, and *Forza Motorsport 7*. And the PS4 had exclusives of its own, with the latest addition to the *Spider-Man* franchise swinging its way onto screens. At the same time, the likes of *Fortnite* and *Overwatch* continued to go from strength to strength, adding awesome new characters and game modes.

Join us as we look back at the highlights of an incredible year of gaming, and look ahead to what's on the horizon . . .

82

108

28

50

50

GREATEST MOMENTS IN GAMING

JOIN US AS WE COUNT DOWN
THE MOST EXCITING, REWARDING,
AND MEMORABLE GAMING
HIGHLIGHTS OF THE YEAR

BEATING BOSSES IN CUPHEAD

50 *Cuphead* is one of the hardest games ever made, but don't despair too much, all it takes is a dose of concentration and memory. As you battle a boss over and over, you'll learn its patterns and attacks. Soon, what once felt impossible can be done without taking a single hit. You can do it!

DID YOU KNOW?

All of the art in *Cuphead* is hand-drawn apart from the color, which is added digitally. What an amazing achievement!

SCORING A KO IN ARMS

49 It may look like a party game, but *Arms* is actually one of the most strategic fighters out there. You have to constantly think in three dimensions, know all your character's specials, and be able to anticipate what's coming your way so that you know how to deal with it. It makes every win feel oh so sweet.

PLAYING AS AKUMA IN TEKKEN 7

48 *Street Fighter* fans have been losing their minds over this one. The series' classic orange-haired demon somehow made his way into *Tekken 7*, and he immediately picked a fight with another crazy-haired dude, Heihachi. Akuma feels amazing to play with too—he even brought his fireballs!

EXPLORING THE HIGH SEAS IN SEA OF THIEVES

47 If you've ever played pirates with your buddies but wanted to take it to the next level, then Rare's enormous *Sea of Thieves* is the game for you! You and your friends can venture out onto the open ocean on a giant galleon, hunt for treasure, discover hidden islands, and, of course, battle other pirates!

GETTING A WINNER ROYALE IN FORTNITE

46 Whether you're playing solo or with friends, nothing beats the feeling of surviving against over 90 opponents and getting that Winner Royale in *Fortnite*. They don't come around very often, so if you do manage to get one, make sure you tell absolutely everybody you know. Photos, emails, letters—whatever it takes!

WINNING THE TITLE IN FIFA 18

45 There are many ways to win in soccer, and many ways to win in *FIFA 18*. You may be an Ultimate Team player and save up all your coins hoping to get Ronaldo, Messi, or Mbappé. Or you may be a tactical genius, working your way up the leagues with a small team in Career Mode. However you win, one thing's for sure, you'll never forget the image of your players celebrating, dancing, smiling, and jumping around with the trophy YOU won.

CREATING A SUPERSTAR IN FIRE PRO WRESTLING WORLD

44 *Fire Pro Wrestling World* doesn't have any real-world grapplers on its roster, so if you want to play as Seth Rollins or Roman Reigns, you're going to have to create them yourself. Thankfully, creating characters is really easy, and you can even download creations from the Steam store. Before you know it, you'll have the biggest collection of wrestlers on the planet.

OUTSMARTING RABBIDS IN MARIO + RABBIDS KINGDOM BATTLE

43 Not many people expected much from a crossover between the Rabbids and Mario, but this is one of the coolest strategy games out there. Those Rabbids are crafty too, so you'll need to use all your skills and some tactical positioning to defeat them.

10:27

EXPERIENCING 4K HDR IN FORZA MOTORSPORT 7

42 Graphics aren't the most important thing in the world, but once you've seen *Forza 7* running in all its glory on the Xbox One X on a 4K TV with HDR, it's difficult to go back to normal gaming. Amazing sunsets, stunning cars, perfect tracks. It's just so beautiful.

RAGING IN GETTING OVER IT

41 If you know what you're doing, you can beat *Getting Over It* in three minutes. But you don't know what you're doing. No one does. This is the year's greatest gaming challenge, a game designed to make you, and your favorite gamers, very angry indeed. Just keep calm, breathe, focus, and you will succeed. Eventually . . .

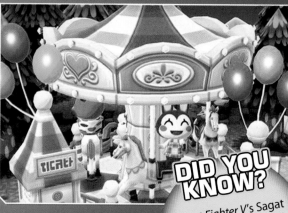

MAKING FRIENDS IN ANIMAL CROSSING: POCKET CAMP

40 *Animal Crossing* always seemed like a great fit for cellphones, and this simple but super cool version works great. It's all about making friends and bringing them presents, while making the most awesome camp site you can, so even more friends come to visit.

DID YOU KNOW?

Street Fighter V's Sagat has been a major part of the series since the original *Street Fighter* way back in 1987.

CRUSHING THE COMPETITION WITH OLD FAVORITES IN STREET FIGHTER V

39 Sagat was the most overpowered character in *Street Fighter IV*, and one of the bosses of the original games, and now he's back. With his brutal range of Tiger attacks, Sagat is just as monstrous as ever. It's good to have him back, unless you have to face him.

GOING BACK INTO SPACE IN METROID: SAMUS RETURNS

38 Any *Metroid* game is a welcome treat, but a 2-D *Metroid*? That's just magical. This 3DS remake of the ancient *Metroid 2* is just as puzzling, exciting, and action-packed as ever, and you'll need both quick reactions and a sharp mind to conquer its maze of space stations and weird alien worlds. Samus, we've missed you.

BACK TO THE RACES IN MARIO KART 8 DELUXE

37 It's been an amazing year for the Switch, so much so that it's easy to forget about this, the finest version of one of the greatest racing games of all time. Online or off, single-player or against your buddies, this is *MK* at its absolute best. There's even a brand-new battle mode so you can compete with your friends for true *Mario Kart* supremacy.

GOING CRAZY WITH DOOMFIST IN OVERWATCH

36 Every time a new character is introduced to *Overwatch*, the player base gets excited, because it means all the classic strategies are about to change. No one could have prepared for Doomfist though, and his giant, well, fist! He brings absolute carnage to every round, and a nice change of pace from all those sneaky snipers!

TACKLING SALMON RUN IN SPLATOON 2

35 What happens when you mix the awesome shooting of *Splatoon* with a wave-based horde mode? You get the incredible Salmon Run! You and three buddies, or random teammates, have to defend your little Grizzco fishing platform from waves of nasty Salmonids, including huge bosses. Survive, and you get tons of XP. Fail, and you'll just go home stinking of fish. It's tense, exciting, super-fast, and always hilarious. Just watch out for those scary Maws—they're deadly!

FRISBEE THROWING IN
WINDJAMMERS

33 It might look like an old game (it is), but this remaster of arcade classic *Windjammers* is as amazing to play now as it was back in the 90s. It's so simple—two players battle back and forth, trying to throw the frisbee past each other. That's it. But it's so fast, so responsive, and so exciting that you may just flip.

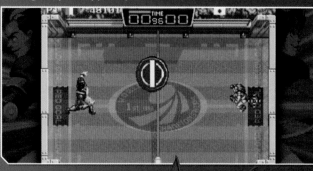

PLAYING ROCKET LEAGUE
ANYWHERE ON THE MOVE

34 Surely there's no way of improving one of the best games of all time, right? Wrong! Now *Rocket League* is available on Nintendo Switch, you can play it literally anywhere. On a train. On a plane. Up a tree! And it's as smooth and fast on Switch as it is anywhere else—you can even compete against Xbox and PC players.

MEETING SHOVEL KNIGHT IN
YOOKA-LAYLEE

32 These indie game makers like to make friends with each other. What a surprise, then, in *Yooka-Laylee*'s gorgeous opening level, to see our old friend Shovel Knight in there, completely lost, and rendered in full 3-D for the first time. You have to help him get back home. More guest characters in games, please!

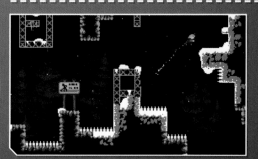

CLIMBING THE MOUNTAIN
IN CELESTE

31 When the creator of the brilliant *TowerFall Ascension* makes a single-player platforming quest, you know you should be paying attention. Celeste has to climb an enormous mountain made up of very tricky platform challenges, and has to use every bit of skill and technique she has to get up there. An indie classic.

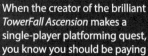

PLAYING MINECRAFT IN 4K

30 Steve and friends have never looked better. It's the same *Minecraft* gameplay that we know and love, but on Xbox One X, the game truly shines. Those blocks have never been sharper, the draw distance has never been longer, and the Creepers have never been scarier. And that's not all—the Better Together Update now lets players on Xbox, mobile, VR, and Windows 10 enjoy *Minecraft* together!

MEETING THE GUARDIANS IN LEGO MARVEL SUPER HEROES 2

29 Any time you're hanging out with Star-Lord, Drax, Rocket Raccoon, and Gamora is a good time. Add Baby Groot into the mix, and you've got yourself a party. LEGO *Marvel Super Heroes 2* doesn't waste much time in letting you play with the whole galactic crew, and the results are just as awesome as you'd expect.

GETTING A HOLE IN ONE IN GOLF STORY

28 Getting a hole in one in any golf game is a big achievement, but nailing one in a golf game that's also a very funny RPG—well, it doesn't get much better than that. *Golf Story* is one of the surprise hits on the Switch so far, and even though its swing mechanic is pretty old-school, it still feels amazing when the ball rattles straight into the hole.

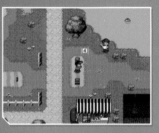

GETTING BIG IN KNACK 2

27 Knack may look like he's made out of shiny nachos, but his weird body can absorb hundreds of extra particles and he can grow as tall as a skyscraper. In *Knack 2*, he gets bigger than ever before, so anything that dares to get in his way ends up swatted aside like a fly at a barbecue.

THE EXPERT SAYS . . .
GAVIN PRINCE
Studio Director, Playtonic

Golf Story on Nintendo Switch is my highlight. It's a superb blend of accessible golfing action and SNES-style RPG-ing that anyone with an interest in either should check out. I loved how the mechanics of shot-taking were repurposed for digging up and collecting items, throwing your balls around, and tee-ing up anywhere is such simple but pure fun. The story and characters are consistently brilliant, the writing is incredibly witty and had me laughing throughout. There are so many neat things to discover including using the wildlife to your advantage, hidden crazy golf, and frisbee golf. It's the must-have golf game I never knew I craved until I played it!

CRAFTING GEAR IN PORTAL KNIGHTS

26 Many games offer adventure. Quite a few games these days let you build your own defenses while you're on that adventure, like *Fortnite* and *Minecraft*. But not many games let you craft your own weapons and shields from what you find in the world. *Portal Knights* lets you do it all, and will have you adventuring for hours and hours.

BATTLING JUAN FROM GUACAMELEE IN BRAWLOUT

25 Another guest character! The excellent Juan—lead character in the awesome platform brawler *Guacamelee*—appears in platform fighter *Brawlout*. Juan is fast, agile, but most importantly, very strong. He's still obsessed with chickens too, as you can hear when he busts out a special move. Olé!

LAUGHING UNCONTROLLABLY IN GANG BEASTS

24 If you've never experienced *Gang Beasts*, then you've never had the joy of seeing four jelly-baby-looking characters flail around in combat, falling about the place and into each other, and trying to push one another off the map. It's non-stop laughs. Just don't expect *Street Fighter*-like precision!

TRYING OUT ALL YOUR OLD GAMES ON XBOX ONE X

23 One of the coolest features of the Xbox One X is backwards compatibility. If you are old enough to have some original Xbox games, and a big collection of Xbox 360 games, you can play most of them on the X, and amazingly, a lot of them will play in 4K, so they look better than ever. Microsoft and the Xbox Team have done amazing work, making the Xbox One X feel like the ultimate games console for Xbox fans.

BUILDING EVERYTHING IN LEGO WORLDS

22 Another building game, but this time it's from the series that's always been obsessed with blocks. LEGO *Worlds* lets you go wild and free with your imagination, so you can build anything that comes to mind using its easy crafting tools and a whole world of little bumpy blocks.

RACING IN VR IN GRAN TURISMO SPORT

21 *Gran Turismo* has always been realistic, but things are taken to a completely different level when you pop on the PlayStation VR headset and actually go inside the cars. It's an intense experience, so probably best not to try for too long, but it's also one you'll never forget, unless you can afford a real supercar one day!

HANGING OUT WITH YOUR HEROES IN SONIC FORCES

20 Sonic, Tails, Knuckles, and even Shadow are back together in this lightning-fast action platformer, but that's not all. For the first time in a *Sonic* game, you can create your own character and join in the fun. Finally, a chance to actually go to Green Hill Zone and experience all that speed for yourself!

MAKING FRIENDS IN THE SIMS 4

19 Maybe you like to create a happy family, where the parents have nine-to-five jobs and the kids go to school. Or maybe you prefer a family of clowns who spend all day causing mischief. Whatever it is you want to do, *The Sims 4* will let you and it's now better than ever. Your Sims have their own moods and personalities, while PC players can even introduce cats and dogs into their worlds.

SCORING A TOUCHDOWN IN MADDEN NFL 18

18 It's always been fun to cross the line into the endzone in *Madden NFL*, but now you can experience it in amazing 4K on Xbox One X, and it looks and feels better than ever. This year's game has an amazing story mode too—*Madden* has never been this good.

ROCKING OUT TO DESPACITO IN JUST DANCE 2018

17 It may have been overplayed, but you know you want to shake it to Bieber and co. in the comfort of your living room. Whether you're playing on Switch, PS4, Xbox, or even PC, *Just Dance 2018* still delivers that combination of hilarious dancing and a huge library of tunes to get the whole family up and boogying.

CATCHING 'EM ALL IN POKÉMON ULTRA SUN AND ULTRA MOON

16 Yes, it's just an updated version of *Pokémon Sun* and *Moon*, but that also means it's an updated version of the greatest *Pokémon* games in years. And if you haven't experienced one of these two amazing games yet, then there is no better time than now. Pack your bags, head to Alola and start hunting for those cute little monsters.

EXPLODING YOUR FRIENDS IN WORMS W.M.D

15 This brilliant updated version of the classic multiplayer game is even available on Nintendo Switch, so you can climb, jump, and squeak your way to victory in the best-looking and deepest version of *Worms* to date. There's even a lengthy single-player mode if the idea of competitive *Worms* doesn't do it for you.

FINDING YOUR INNER WARRIOR IN THE LEGO NINJAGO MOVIE VIDEO GAME

14 The LEGO games have always featured combat, but in *The LEGO Ninjago Movie Video Game*, there are more moves than ever. There are also clips from the film in between levels, so you can be smashing bad guys one minute and laughing your head off the next.

LAUGHING AND JUMPING IN A HAT IN TIME

13 One of the best 3-D platformers in years, *A Hat in Time* mixes great gameplay with funny characters and imaginative level design. One of the best levels sees you sneaking into a movie studio to make your own film and get a huge new fan base, all while mischievous robots try to stop you.

GORGEOUS PLATFORMING IN SUPER LUCKY'S TALE

12 One of the Xbox One X's hidden gems, *Super Lucky's Tale* may look like a simple platform game, but it's actually full of creative levels, smart gameplay ideas, and heaps of humor and charm. If you're a fan of 3-D platformers, then what a year you're having—be sure not to miss out.

SPEED RACING IN SONIC MANIA

11 Two *Sonic* games in one year— what a speedy treat! This is a throwback to the classic *Sonic* games from the 90s, and it's actually created by a *Sonic* superfan who used all the knowledge gained from his years and years of playing the series to create something original. The team at SEGA employed him to make his own game, and this is what he came up with, a magical experience that fans both young and old absolutely adore, and one that's been hailed as the best *Sonic* game in over 20 years. What other series should get a sequel made by a fan?

DID YOU KNOW?

One of *Sonic Mania's* bosses actually turns into a version of *Dr. Robotnik's Mean Bean Machine*, a puzzle game from the 90s!

SCORE
TIME 0
RINGS

© 2018 The LEGO Group. ™ & © WBEI

GETTING CARTOONY IN
NI NO KUNI II

10 The original *Ni no Kuni* was a gorgeous and huge Japanese RPG from the amazing minds at Level-5. We didn't really expect a sequel, so what a great surprise to be given another massive, beautiful, and deep experience to get stuck into. Wonderful characters, stunning graphics, and incredible music await.

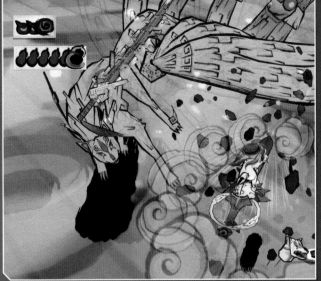

PAINTING IN OKAMI HD

09 *Okami* is an absolutely stunning adventure that mixes the exploration and puzzles of *Zelda* with an amazing painted world that looks like traditional Japanese artwork. You play as Amaterasu, a wolf goddess who uses a magical paintbrush to destroy her enemies with ink. It's a truly memorable experience.

GOING PINK IN KIRBY
BATTLE ROYALE

08 No, the chubby pink guy isn't heading into the wilds of *Fortnite* to do battle with 99 other players, this isn't that kind of Battle Royale. He is, however, getting into some fun and frantic sword fights in this charming story-driven battler on 3DS. The combat is fast and surprisingly deep, and it's as fun and friendly as ever.

SOLVING PUZZLES
IN RIME

07 Many people have compared this gorgeous exploration game to *Journey*, and it's easy to see why. *Rime* is different, though, as it asks players to solve some pretty crazy puzzles in order to get through its mysterious sand-filled world. *Rime* isn't the most action-packed game this year, but it is one of the most interesting and thought-provoking. And it looks stunning.

EXPLORING THE WONDER OF XENOBLADE CHRONICLES 2

06 Wow, what a year the Nintendo Switch has had. Alongside all the big first-party Nintendo games, here we have a giant 100-hour-plus RPG that lets you explore huge worlds, some of which are actually on the backs of giant creatures! There's nothing quite like *Xenoblade Chronicles 2*, and Switch owners should absolutely check it out.

GOING SUPER SAIYAN IN DRAGON BALL FIGHTERZ

05 There have been *Dragon Ball Z* games for many years, but never like this. Arc System Works' amazing 2-D fighter looks absolutely incredible, plays faster than any other fighting game out there, and captures the madcap mania of the TV show while never being too overwhelming for players. Kaio-ken!

PLAYING WITH TRICO IN VR IN THE LAST GUARDIAN VR

03 *The Last Guardian* is a one-of-a-kind experience, but trying to get the giant bird-dragon Trico to do what you want can be painful at times. Now, though, you can don a PlayStation VR headset and hang out with your fluffy, feathery friend whenever you want. It's a short experience, but mind-blowing all the same, and a great example of VR done well.

GETTING CREATIVE WITH NINTENDO LABO

04 Nintendo brought the Switch to life and set imaginations running free with the release of its Labo construction kits. Turn sheets of cardboard into a variety of cool shapes – from a toy piano to a robot – then combine your creations with your Switch to create the ultimate interactive gaming experience. Welcome to the future of gaming!

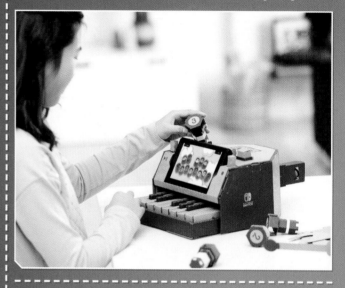

BATTLING CALAMITY GANON IN THE LEGEND OF ZELDA: BREATH OF THE WILD

02 After nearly a hundred hours of exploration, shrines, cooking, slipping in the rain, and fighting with Bokoblins, it all comes down to this. Charging Hyrule Castle, defeating the Guardians, fighting your way into the center, and battling the nightmare itself: Calamity Ganon. It's a tough fight, but if you've enlisted the help of the four divine beasts along the way, you can make short work of this evil demon. *Breath of the Wild's* final showdown is sensational.

GOING BACK TO THE MUSHROOM KINGDOM IN SUPER MARIO ODYSSEY

01

Well, here it is. The most epic moment in the last year of gaming, from a game filled to the brim with amazing moments. You've battled through the Cascade Kingdom, conquered New Donk City, and turned into meat in the Luncheon Kingdom. You've become a T-Rex, a Chain Chomp, a Goomba, and even a Hammer Bro. And when you finally defeat Bowser, rescue Peach, and save the world once again, where do you go? Well, home of course!

Visiting the Mushroom Kingdom in *Super Mario Odyssey* is an amazing experience, because it's a perfect throwback to Peach's Castle in *Super Mario 64*. Here, though, there are secrets everywhere. Have you climbed onto the roof and found your old pal Yoshi? How about stacking all the Goombas in the forest, or helping Toad plant seeds in his garden?

The whole level feels like a gift for Mario fans—a truly amazing way to finish one of the greatest games of all time.

DID YOU KNOW?

If you get to 500 moons in *Super Mario Odyssey*, you unlock the final challenge and can see the true ending.

👍 DID YOU SEE THAT?!

DID YOU SEE THAT?!

CRASH BANDICOOT

The *N. Sane Trilogy* brought Crash back looking better than ever and with a few additions. *Crash 1, 2,* and *3* all now feature Time Trial modes. After beating a level, you can replay it, collect the stopwatch and try to beat the level as quickly as possible. Platinum relics are awarded for beating the game's best time. You'll have to run, spin and jump like never before to beat these times, but here are some tips for getting the best times.

1 Not only do the yellow boxes stop time, but they are also always placed along the fastest route of the map. So as you go along the level make sure to destroy them along the way. If you miss one of them, sometimes making another attempt to break it will be worthwhile.

2 Grab the Aku Aku masks as you go. Some levels have spots where taking a hit can be much quicker than avoiding the enemy all together. Just like the time boxes, these are always placed along the fastest route of the map.

22 GAME ON! 2019

3 This tip only applies to *Crash 2* and *3*. Press the slide button quickly followed by the spin button to perform a spin slide. To get over larger gaps and make shortcuts press the slide button followed by jump and spin in quick succession.

4 Expect to die. A lot. There is a lot of trial and error that comes with doing these time trials. However, you don't lose lives when you're in time trials, so you can try new methods without worrying about getting a game over.

SPIDER-MAN

WITH GREAT POWER . . .

Your friendly neighborhood Spider-Man swings into action on the PlayStation 4 for a console-exclusive adventure that will blow you away. Developed by Insomniac Games, *Spider-Man* offers the adventure of a lifetime. It'll be here that you learn the true meaning of Spidey's mantra "With great power . . . comes great responsibility." You're going to apply this saying as you swing across a huge open-world city, as you fight against bad guys and send them off to jail, and do your best to keep New York City safe from evil forces. If you're a fan of the comics, the films, or just the character in general, trust us; this is going to be the best *Spider-Man* game that has ever been made.

STATS

The first Spider-Man game came out **36** YEARS AGO

Features **3** playable characters

PETER PARKER IS **23**

Spidey is **8** YEARS into his career as the wall crawler

PICTURES OF SPIDER-MAN

WELCOME TO NYC

Spider-Man is going to be set in an open-world version of Marvel's New York City. That means you'll be able to swing freely around it and you might even run into some familiar faces along the way—we've already caught a glimpse of Doctor Strange's Sanctum Sanctorum.

COSTUME CHANGE

The longer you play, the more opportunities you'll have to upgrade Peter's gadgets, combat abilities, and clothing. The game is going to be packed with classic and cool collectibles!

INTO THE ACTION

This isn't the Spider-Man that you saw in *Homecoming*. Instead, this game will depict the famed superhero a handful of years into his career. That means he's going to be more capable and more awesome than you've ever seen him in a video game before.

FREE-FLOWING COMBAT

Spidey has always been an acrobatic improviser and that's captured in this game. With free-flowing combat, you'll be able to chain combos together utilizing everything from the environments to a wide array of gadgets to take down the bad guys and masked villains running wild on the streets of Manhattan.

TIPS & TRICKS

Pay attention
Spider-Man's webs actually attach to the buildings, so you always need to be sure that there is one in sight to continue swinging around.

Use the environment
Spidey isn't the strongest hero, so you'll need to use the environments to get one up on his foes.

Remember your gadgets
Instead of fighting multiple enemies at the same time why not use your gadgets to try and dispatch them all at once?

Work/life balance
There's more to *Spider-Man* than swinging around. Remember to check in with M.J. and Harry Osborn for missions.

Eyes open
Keep your eyes open for collectibles strewn across the city. Finding these will help you unlock cool new costumes and secrets.

THE DEV SPEAKS

BRYAN INTIHAR

Who?
Bryan Intihar is the creative director at Insomniac Games, the team behind *Spider-Man*.

On the new *Spider-Man*...
"This is a concrete jungle gym that Spider-Man is flying through. We obviously want to have a level of accessibility but then also some skill to it as well. And since this is Spider-Man eight years into his career, there's a sense of experience with Peter doing this. When it comes to combat, I think it's the improvisational nature of him. To us, he's not a brawler; he's more of an acrobatic improviser. It's really leveraging the idea of him being able to look at a situation and blending between melee, using his webs, environment reaction—reading the room to see what he can do, as well as mixing in gadgets. It's really about Spider-Man being able to switch between those elements as fast as possible. For me, I think that's really important."

Inner Demons
These are the henchmen of Mister Negative; wearing dragon-style masks, they usually come equipped with a whole host of super sharp weaponry to fight you with.

COOLEST ENEMIES

Mister Negative
The main villain in *Spider-Man*, Mister Negative is a powerful foe who not only has super strength but the power to harness dark energy against his enemy (that's you, BTW)!

DID YOU KNOW?
Mary Jane Watson will of course make an appearance. She's working as a reporter for the Daily Bugle and will have her own playable sections!

ALSO CHECK OUT . . .

Spider-Man: Shattered Dimensions
Realities collide in *Spider-Man: Shattered Dimensions*, a fun game that lets players control four very different versions of the web slinger from all across the extended Marvel universe that we know.

DID YOU KNOW?

Miles Morales is going to be in the game, but will he get into his own Spidey suit to help Peter Parker fight crime? We can only hope so!

THE EXPERT SAYS . . .
JOSH WEST
Deputy Editor, games™ magazine

This is the ultimate *Spider-Man* game, the one that oh-so-many fans of the web swinger have spent decades waiting to play and enjoy. Developer Insomniac (famed for its work on *Spyro the Dragon* and *Ratchet & Clank*) has nailed the feel and look of the world, it's a playground designed to let you indulge in the acrobatic movement and super-stylish combat that Spider-Man is known for. Add in a bunch of quippy one-liners and smart mission design to the mixture and you're looking at a *Spider-Man* game no fans of the character, or action-adventure games in general, should dare miss out on.

Shocker
A classic *Spider-Man* villain enters the fray in the form of Shocker. Don't get too close to him, he can fire powerful electro-shockwaves from his fists!

Kingpin
It wouldn't be a *Spider-Man* game without the appearance of New York City secret overlord Kingpin. Expect him to cause some chaos.

The Amazing Spider-Man 2
The Amazing Spider-Man 2 is another sprawling Spidey game, only this one has been designed to tie-in with Andrew Garfield's 2014 *Spider-Man* movie of the same name.

Spider-Man 2
This retro *Spider-Man* game might not be a looker but it's one of the best games to ever feature the wall crawler. It features a big world to explore, awesome swinging, and a really cool roster of villains to punch in the face.

DID YOU KNOW?

Kirby: Star Allies greatly resembles the cancelled *Kirby GCN*, which was originally intended for release on the Nintendo GameCube.

FRIEND OR FOE?
KIRBY: STAR ALLIES

HAL Laboratory's loveable pink blob has been entertaining gamers for over 25 years, so it makes sense that his latest adventure has come to Nintendo Switch.

As with previous *Kirby* games, the coolest aspect of *Star Allies* is that you can suck up any enemy, and copy their unique abilities.

Kirby is able to mix abilities by inhaling two different enemies, and even gain the abilities of special helpers that will come to his aid as he embarks on his colorful quest. The big difference this time, though, is that the helper can be controlled by another player. It's also possible to mix helpers with abilities, which will create all sorts of crazy situations for the loveable pink hero.

STATS

4 players can play at once

It's been 21 YEARS since Nago, Pitch, and ChuChu have been in a *Kirby* game

1992 IS WHEN THE FRANCHISE FIRST STARTED

Over 20 fun helpers

TOP 5 KIRBY GAMES

Kirby's greatest adventures

KIRBY'S EPIC YARN

1 This delightful game has Kirby transformed into a piece of magic yarn, which enables him to turn into all sorts of useful forms, from a missile-launching robot to an incredibly useful submarine. Unfortunately, for Kirby, being made out of a piece of yarn means he can no longer fly or inhale enemies. What a shame.

KIRBY SUPER STAR ULTRA

2 This is actually eight games in one. The main game is a remake of Kirby's original Game Boy adventure, *Kirby's Dream Land*, while the other offerings are crazy minigames that range from racing against King Dedede to exploring a huge cave full of treasure.

KIRBY: CANVAS CURSE

3 The first DS *Kirby* game lets you use your stylus to draw routes. Poking Kirby with the stylus causes him to dash; poking enemies stuns them, giving him time to run away or bash into them. Sequel *Kirby and the Rainbow Curse* is available on Wii U.

KIRBY: PLANET ROBOBOT

4 One of the best *Kirby* games is on 3DS and allows Kirby to climb into a robot suit. He's still able to suck up enemies and use their abilities, but the suit has lots of clever powers that allow him to manipulate his environment. Special editions come with a cute Amiibo.

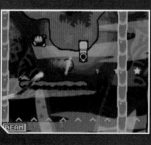

KIRBY MASS ATTACK

5 What's better than a game with one Kirby in it? A game with lots of Kirbies! *Mass Attack* is another fun DS game that has you flicking loads of Kirbies at your enemies to stop them in their tracks or solve puzzles. It also has some sensational boss fights.

TIPS & TRICKS

Suck 'em up
Do not be afraid to suck up enemies whenever you see them—it's the safest way to avoid them.

Mix and match
Always suck up different enemies when you can, because you'll never know what type of cool ability you'll end up with.

Boss rush
While *Kirby* bosses are often easy, they still have attack patterns that need to be mastered. Watch carefully to discover their weaknesses.

Team up
Kirby: Star Allies is designed to be played with friends so you'll get the best results by teaming up with your buddies.

Fly Kirby, fly
If there's too much action on the ground then don't be afraid to take to the air in order to avoid your enemies.

SEA OF THIEVES

PIRATE'S LIFE FOR YOU

If you're looking to have the adventure of a lifetime then you are going to want to get involved with *Sea of Thieves*. It's the latest title from legendary British game developer Rare, responsible for old retro classics like *Banjo-Kazooie* and *Donkey Kong Country*, which lets you and your friends become pirate legends. Form a crew, navigate the seas in your own customizable vessel, and search the huge open world for buried treasure to unearth, ancient creatures to defeat in combat, and other real players to challenge in epic pirate-ship battles. *Sea of Thieves* is one of the most exciting games available on the Xbox One and PC; it's about having fun with your friends, building your own pirate adventures, and exploring the mysteries of the sea.

STATS

4 PLAYERS PER SHIP

3 different pirate factions to join ☠ ☠ ☠

1.2 MILLION+ E3 2017 TRAILER VIEWS ON You**Tube**

100+ DIFFERENT QUESTS AND VOYAGES

TOP 5 THINGS TO TRY

Make your game more exciting!

GO SOLO

1 If you want to build your own legendary reputation, you can hit the seas by yourself rather than with a crew. *Sea of Thieves* includes small vessels that you can navigate solo. Fast and easy to pilot, these ships ensure it's still super-fun to tackle the game on your own. Besides, find treasure on your own and you won't have to give a cut of it to your friends!

GET CREATIVE

2 If you can see another ship on the horizon that you want to reach, or you want to make it over to a distant island before everybody else gets there, all you need to do is get a little bit creative. Have a go at loading yourself into a cannon and firing yourself across huge distances! Not only does it save time, but you'll soon discover that it's a really great tactic should you want to make a surprise entrance.

FIND TREASURE

4 Treasure maps can be purchased at small trading villages and towns, and yes, X does indeed mark the spot. You'll need to follow the clues to the letter if you want to unearth the loot though; working with your friends to find some smartly hidden chests is a must!

BE YOURSELF

5 The more you play *Sea of Thieves*, the more you are able to build your legendary status, which will allow you to unlock a whole host of really cool items. We're talking unique and rare costumes, new songs that you can play on your musical instruments, and really fun ways to make your ship stand out on the open seas.

FORM A CREW

3 *Sea of Thieves* supports two- and four-player play-sessions, with each ship class gradually becoming more difficult to use and maintain. That's all part of the fun of it though; get a group together and sail one of the larger ships successfully, and you'll feel like a true pirate!

ALSO CHECK OUT . . .

Minecraft

When it comes to having fun with your buddies, it doesn't get much better than *Minecraft*. Get into a new world and start building out your own adventures. Anything is possible with a little imagination and hard work.

Guns of Icarus Online

This online MMO is *Sea of Thieves* in the skies; steampunk airships float through the air, maintained by other players, all of whom are looking to battle and trade valuable resources.

TOP 10 MULTIPLAYER GAMES

Rocket League

1 The emperor of multiplayer. *Rocket League* is perfection—car-based soccer with incredible action, fast-paced fun, a learning curve that's easy to pick up and hard to master, and some of the most competitive matches we've ever seen in a game. Whether you're playing locally or online, you're absolutely guaranteed a good time. And with all manner of new vehicles added—like the Batmobile!—you're sure to always find a car that suits your tastes.

Overwatch

2 Not only is *Overwatch* one of the best multiplayer games, it's one of the best games period. A team-based online battle sees players picking characters with a wide variety of different strengths and weaknesses, then working together to best the other team and come out on top. Or working as a group of individuals and ending up on the losing side . . .

Overcooked!

3 Get some friends around the console, hand out the controllers, and get to work on some hardcore cooking action. *Overcooked!* is frantic, over-the-top fun for gamers of all ages and skill levels, and it's the kind of thing that gets players talking to—or screaming at—each other. It's about as stressful as working in a real kitchen, but definitely a lot more fun.

6 WAYS TO BE A GREAT PLAYER ONLINE

1 STICK TO THE RULES
There are times when it's tempting to bend the rules a bit to your advantage, but who wants a victory tainted by such behavior? Stick to the rules and learn the game—get better that way and it's much more satisfying.

4 INVITE OTHERS TO PLAY
We all have our squads online and friends in local multiplayer to play with regularly, but you can make the experience even better by inviting friends of your friends into your game. Who knows—you might make a new friend out of it!

2 CONGRATULATE EVERYONE
There's nothing great about gloating when you win, and there's nothing great about mocking those who did poorly. Play positively, behave well and congratulate everyone for playing—it's just a game, after all!

5 TRY DIFFERENT CHARACTERS/LOADOUTS
It's tempting to stick with what you know, but if you venture out of your comfort zone you'll have a lot more fun learning the game's systems and how things interact with other players.

3 WORK TOGETHER
Teamwork isn't always the way—look at *Tekken*, for example. But in games when you can work as a team, you really should. Not only is it more fun to work together; you'll actually end up playing better if you do so.

6 HELP OTHER PLAYERS
Not everyone will be as good as other players, so it's up to those of us who are better to help others improve. If they're better, the game is more fun, they have more fun, we have more fun, everything's more fun!

Destiny 2

4 If you're looking for a game to slow things down a bit and play with a committed group of friends online, look no further than *Destiny 2*. The setting might not be for everyone, but those who get drawn into its world won't be leaving any time soon. It's compelling and great fun, with a sense of wonder you don't find many other places.

Mario Kart 8 Deluxe

5 How could a list of multiplayer greats be complete without *Mario Kart*? And, fortunately, *Mario Kart 8 Deluxe* on Switch is the definitive version of one of the best multiplayer games ever made. It's classic karting action with all the Nintendo characters and stages you love, and all the weapons you don't.

Nidhogg 2

6 It looks weird, but *Nidhogg 2* is a brilliant game to play with friends. Basically it's a swordfighting game. Less basically, it's a swordfighting game full of skill, tactics, and incredible speed—all played out in a hyperactive world that doesn't let you stop to catch your breath at any point. Alone, it's merely okay. With friends, it's incredible.

Tekken 7

7 The good old fighting game genre wouldn't be where it is today without the likes of *Tekken*, so it's brilliant to see the latest game in the series still has all the multiplayer quality you would expect from such heritage. You can play online, but the real draw is playing against someone in the same room. That's the real challenge.

Star Wars Battlefront II

8 *Battlefront II* offers the best looking, most in-depth online multiplayer version of the galaxy far, far away. Pick from characters across all eras, battle in arenas based on your favorite locations and generally have a lot of fun in huge, over-the-top battles for galactic supremacy.

Jackbox Party Pack series

9 Sometimes you need an old-fashioned quiz game to keep everyone happy. Fortunately, the *You Don't Know Jack* folks have been releasing a bunch of updated Jackbox content packs to keep you quizzing, guessing, and hooting with delight. These are designed not so much for your hardcore gamers—there are no scorestreaks here—but the Jackbox series is still a lot of fun for everyone.

Splatoon 2

10 Another multiplayer great from Nintendo, *Splatoon 2* takes the formula of the original game and improves it in many ways. In short, you have to paint the whole arena your team's color while switching between human and squid form—which sounds silly, but is actually amazingly good fun. Get a good group of friends on this one and you won't want to put it down.

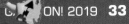

THE GAME WITH SOMETHING FOR EVERYONE

LIGHTSEEKERS: AWAKENING

With so many amazing toys-to-life games getting canceled now, it's fantastic to see that the genre lives on in the form of the excellent Kickstarter-funded *Lightseekers: Awakening.* As with the likes of *Skylanders, Disney Infinity,* and LEGO *Dimensions, Lightseekers* features cool, collectible models that come to life when you use them in the free downloadable action game that's available. Oh, and unlike similar games there's no need for a portal, as all the clever technology is Bluetooth-enabled. It's great seeing your favorite heroes come to life in video game form, but *Lightseekers* goes one better than other similar games as there is also a cool trading card game that's equally great fun to play. The cards can also be used to deliver augmented reality experiences and bonuses when playing the *Lightseekers* video game as well, meaning you get fantastic value for money.

STATS

Over **385** collectible cards

There are currently **4** ✓✓✓✓ STARTER PACKS TO COLLECT

Lightseekers raised **$227,660** on Kickstarter

1,635 — fans backed it —

TOP 5 HEROES OF LIGHTSEEKERS

IRONBARK

1 Sergeant Ironbark is a master of the Nature order and uses the Animal, Forest and Soul elements. He is extremely skilled in combat and makes for a formidable foe in battle. He comes in the form of a rare card in the collectible card game and has 30 life points.

ZYRUS

2 Zyrus is a member of the Noxin race and not someone to mess with. He specializes in the Dread order and uses the elements of Poison, Death, and Shadow to confound his enemies. Zyrus is also a rare card in the collectible card game with 31 life points.

DID YOU KNOW?

Lightseekers figures are made by Tomy and are highly poseable. Best of all, they light up, talk, and vibrate during play.

ELARA

5 This clever member of the Yikona tribe is as skilled in battle as she is wise, which makes for a deadly combination. She has worked hard to obtain mastery of the Astral order, which specializes in the elements of Solar, Lunar, and Gravity. She's a rare card and has 30 life points.

KORA

3 This exceptionally cheerful Mari can see the best of any bad situation and is very useful to have in battle. She uses the Storm order to her advantage and has mastery of the Water, Lightning, and Air elements. Her collectible card is rare and she has 28 life points.

JAX

4 If you want to play someone with access to amazing gadgets then Jax is your Tyrax of choice. He is incredibly gifted at using the Tech order and can utilize Mechanical, Time, and Explosives elements to his advantage. He's another rare card in the CCG, with 30 life points.

TIPS & TRICKS

Go big
Bigger challenges will be harder to complete but they do offer far better rewards that pay off in the long run.

Additional extras
Buying new physical items and accessories for your heroes translates into cool new weapons to use in the game.

Master bosses
Bosses can look tough, but they typically have a weakness if you look hard enough and give great bonuses when defeated.

Pay attention
Lightseekers is set in a world filled with the expected lore and tips, so make sure you listen when characters speak to you.

Be flexible
Lightseekers has a flexible combat engine that can be tailored to how you like to play. Get to know it and its advantages.

DID YOU KNOW?

Intelligent Systems and Nintendo originally planned for *Fire Emblem Awakening* to be the last game in the series.

NINTENDO'S FRANCHISE KEEPS ON GIVING

FIRE EMBLEM

It's been a fantastic time for *Fire Emblem* fans lately, with new games on all sorts of systems. *Fire Emblem Heroes* is available on iOS and Android, and is a fun, free-to-play game with premium elements. You can train some of the greatest heroes from *Fire Emblem's* 28-year history after they all collide together in spectacular fashion. *Fire Emblem Warriors* on Switch and 3DS continues the theme of mixing heroes from

different *Fire Emblem* games together, but now the focus is on *Dynasty Warriors*-styled action, and it is fantastic fun. You've also got *Fire Emblem Echoes: Shadows of Valentia*, which is an excellent 3DS remake of one of the earliest games in the series.

Last, but by no means least, is *Fire Emblem Switch*, which is a more traditional *Fire Emblem* game that features the same fun strategy elements that made the 3DS games so fun to play.

STATS

8 Fire Emblem games have been released in the West

Fire Emblem Warriors features **23** PLAYABLE CHARACTERS

There are **16** games in the core series

THE FRANCHISE FIRST BEGAN IN **1990**

TOP 5 FIRE EMBLEM HEROES

The key players you *need* to be aware of!

1 MARTH

Marth is one of *Fire Emblem*'s most popular characters, as he first appeared in the original Famicom adventure. He gained popularity in the West when he appeared in *Super Smash Bros. Melee* on GameCube. He's appeared in several different *Fire Emblem* games and remains a real fan favorite.

2 CHROM

This handsome prince is a more recent member of the *Fire Emblem* franchise, having first appeared in *Fire Emblem Awakening* for 3DS. He's actually a very distant relative of Marth, and is the captain of an elite fighting force called the Shepherds. He also pops up in *Tokyo Mirage Sessions #FE*.

3 LYNDIS

Also known by her nickname, Lyn, Lyndis is one of three heroes who star in *Fire Emblem* on the Game Boy Advance. She's a memorable hero, as it was the first *Fire Emblem* game to appear in the West, laying the groundwork for the *Fire Emblem* titles that would follow.

4 IKE

This noble warrior made his first appearance in *Fire Emblem: Path of Radiance* for Nintendo GameCube, and eventually becomes the leader of the Greil Mercenaries. He proved to be such a hit with fans of the franchise that his adventures continued in *Fire Emblem: Radiant Dawn* on Nintendo's Wii.

5 LISSA

She looks cute, but don't mess with her, as this feisty young cleric is the sister of Chrom, and acts as the primary healer for Chrom's group, the Shepherds. Like Chrom, she made her first appearance in *Fire Emblem Awakening* but has gone on to appear in *Fates*, *Heroes*, and *Warriors*.

TIPS & TRICKS

Map methods

Every *Fire Emblem* fight takes place on a map. Study it carefully to ensure you don't get easily trapped.

Weapon triangle

In many *Fire Emblem* games, swords beat axes, axes beat lances, and lances beat swords. Use this to turn battles.

Don't forget healers

You won't get far in *Fire Emblem* without using your healers. They restore health, allowing your warriors to battle on.

Range over melee

You should always use Mages and Archers on the battlefield, as they can attack without fear of retaliation.

Talking is good

You should chat to friendly allies whenever you can, as this gives you useful boosts later in the game.

DID YOU KNOW?

There's a secret lot in Willow Creek called Sylvan Glade. You'll find it by watering the huge tree in the area.

A WHOLE NEW WORLD

THE SIMS 4

After almost 20 years and 200 million games sold around the world, there's still nothing that can beat the true magic of *The Sims.* Now in its fourth outing, this life sim isn't showing any signs of slowing down, and now you can even play on Xbox One and PS4 as well as PC. While the day-to-day of *The Sims* is the same as ever—yes, they still really need the toilet and take regular showers—there's never been a better time to jump in.

Building houses is more fun and detailed than ever before, Sims have their own moods and unique personalities, and you'll never be quite sure what's going to happen next. Plus, if you're playing on PC, you can even give your Sims cats and dogs to play with.

STATS

 Over **5** million copies sold worldwide

123 BREEDS OF DOG IN CATS & DOGS

 **18** YEARS SINCE THE FIRST *SIMS*

THERE ARE **21** EXPANSIONS AND ADD-ONS ON PC

TOP 5 THINGS TO DO

Show your Sims a good time—or a bad one!

PAT SOME GOOD DOGS

1 The new Cats & Dogs add-on for PC means you can fill Sim homes with all kinds of canine and feline friends. You'll have to feed and play with them, and even take them to the vet if they get unwell. It also adds a whole new coastal area called Brindleton Bay to explore.

GET BUILDING

2 Your Sims need a roof over their heads, and with all kinds of exciting build tools, you can choose whether they live the life of luxury in a Hollywood mansion, or in a tiny room with only a picture of a clown for company . . . Yes. Creepy.

FACE UP!

3 Whether you want to create yourself perfectly in Sim form or just fill a house with all of your friends, the Create a Sim screen is an incredible personalization tool. From eyes to mouths and everything in between (yes, that's noses) you can tweak and play to your heart's content.

WORK IT OUT

4 It's time to make some cash to spend on new things for your house. Send your Sim out to work as a scientist, astronaut, doctor, or even eSports hero. Some job types can be done at home while others will require them to get up and head out into the world.

TOO COOL FOR SKULL

5 Sure, you could just bring out the Spooky Stuff add-on at Halloween, but where would the fun in that be? This download for PC adds pumpkin carving, costumes, make-up, and a scary party option. Perfect for making haunted houses.

TIPS & TRICKS

Money, money, money!
On console, press all your triggers and bumpers and enter 'testingcheats on' in the box. Press the same buttons again and type "motherlode" for $50,000!

Moo-ve it
There's a living Cow Plant in the *Sims 4*! To plant your own, the easiest way to find a Cow Plant berry is by fishing in the Forgotten Grotto.

Cash in
Buy the NanoCan Touchless Trash Can and rake in the simoleons just for putting trash in the trash can. You'll get $10 for every member of your household.

Mood news
Take advantage of your Sims' moods. Careers and skills all have an Ideal Mood, so make sure they're feeling right first.

Worked up
You can control exactly how hard your Sim is working. Just click on their portrait while they're away and you can tell them what to do.

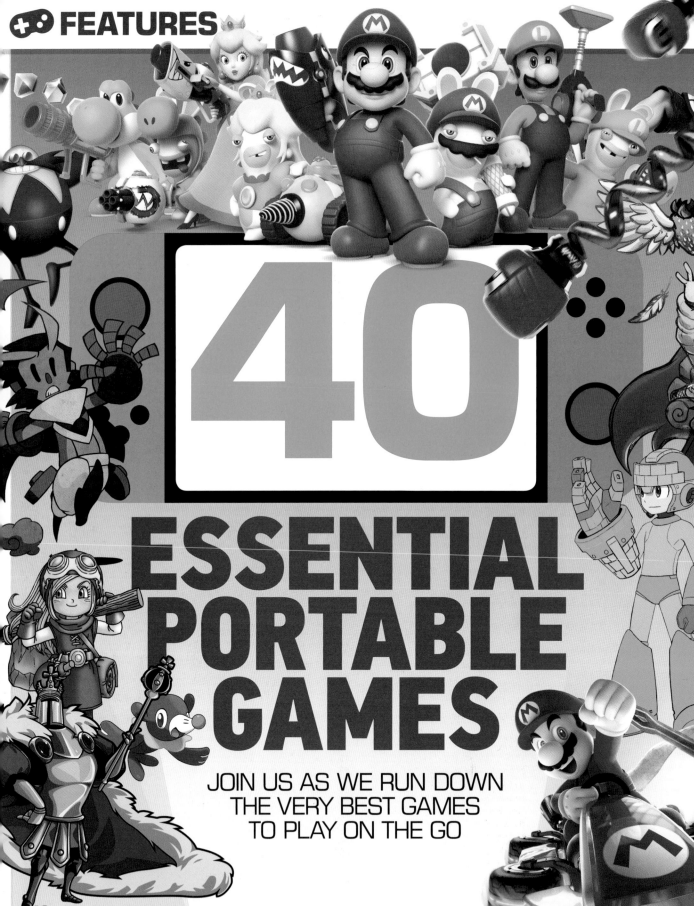

40
ESSENTIAL
PORTABLE
GAMES

JOIN US AS WE RUN DOWN
THE VERY BEST GAMES
TO PLAY ON THE GO

MEGA MAN 11
Nintendo Switch

40 The legendary *Mega Man* is back again. The series has got a new 3-D art style, but it's the same intense and tricky action platforming that *Mega Man's* been doing for decades. There are loads of cool abilities to unlock as rewards for tackling the game's bosses.

TINY WINGS iOS

39 You play as a bird that can't fly, but really wants to, so it uses the hills to launch itself high into the air. *Tiny Wings* is an enjoyable and easy-to-pick-up game—you only need to tap with one finger, the music is relaxing, and it can be played in short bursts.

SILLY WALKS iOS

38 The name says it all: this game is about silly walks. You tap the screen to switch between your character's right and left legs while trying to avoid falling off the edge or hitting dangerous obstacles. Your goal is to save your friends from the evil blender that's come to life and kidnapped them.

DID YOU KNOW?
Developed by Tokyo RPG Factory, *Lost Sphear* is seen as a spiritual successor to the studio's first title, *I Am Setsuna*.

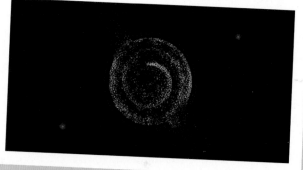

FROST iOS

37 If you're looking for a game to chill out to, then *Frost* is perfect for you. With beautiful glowing visuals and relaxing sounds, *Frost* is a pleasure to play around with. The goal of this puzzler is to guide an orb, or orbs, into a similarly colored light swarm.

CAMPFIRE COOKING iOS

35 Cooking your campfire meal to perfection is the aim of this little puzzle game. It's not just a case of pushing around your marshmallow-laden sticks, or jostling your fondue without thinking. You must plan each move carefully, or you'll end up with a burnt meal!

LOST SPHEAR
Nintendo Switch

36 Kanata is a young man tasked with protecting his town from monsters. He soon has to venture out on a more important quest, however, gathering a party of friends to help him out in the game's turn-based battles. The world is fading, and only Kanata's power of Memory can save it.

RIPTIDE GP: RENEGADE
Android, iOS, Nintendo Switch

34 You can find an endless amount of racing games involving cars, but how many feature armored hydrojets? *Riptide GP: Renegade* lets you ride through old ruins and city waterways, while crashing through obstacles and performing stunts to get first prize. Customize your gear and race with up to four players online.

DANDARA Android, iOS, Nintendo Switch

33 Explore a seemingly endless number of caverns as you fight enemies and discover new power-ups to access previously unreachable places. What makes *Dandara* different is the main character cannot run. You move through the world by jumping from surface to surface—no matter what it is—just as long as it is within your reach!

DRAGON QUEST BUILDERS
Nintendo Switch

32 It's clear that this game about collecting resources, crafting tools, and building, is heavily inspired by *Minecraft*. However, *Dragon Quest Builders* has its own ideas too. The game draws on the series' roots, giving you quests to complete and characters to interact with.

PUMPED BMX Android

31 There are four *Pumped BMX* games on the Android store and in each one you ride through the levels performing tricks to get the highest score in the quickest time possible. The first game alone has over 100 challenges and over 1,000 possible combinations of tricks.

CLASH ROYALE
iOS, Android

30 If you're the kind of player who enjoys collecting and upgrading then you'll love *Clash Royale*. It's a mix of tower defense, multiplayer online battle, and collectible card game. Play online to earn chests that contain new items and boost your equipment, or form clans with your friends to work together, complete quests, climb the ranks online, and unlock better items.

CELESTE Nintendo Switch

29 Made by the team behind the fantastic *TowerFall*, this is a game about climbing a mountain. Watch out for falling blocks and spike pits as you nimbly jump from wall to wall and run across crumbling bridges in this tricky platformer packed full of clever ideas.

POKÉMON GO
iOS, Android

28 An instant hit when it first launched, *Pokémon GO* is still going strong thanks to regular updates. Get out in the real world and discover and catch over 250 Pokémon, battle it out at Gyms, and complete Field Research quests to get your hands on some truly legendary Pokémon. Can you catch them all?

ARKANOID VS SPACE INVADERS
iOS, Android

27 Two retro classics are fused together for this cool game: the ball bouncing, block smashing gameplay of *Arkanoid*, and the alien-destroying shooting of *Space Invaders*. There are both aliens and blocks on screen and you have to bounce alien fire back towards them to clear each level.

SUPERBROTHERS: SWORD & SWORCERY EP
Android, iOS

26 In this excellent adventure game you travel up a mountain and through ruins. While there is combat, the emphasis is on atmosphere, style, and exploration. You control your character by tapping on where you would like them to go, while certain in-game events depend on what phase the moon is in in the real world.

DID YOU KNOW?
Superbrothers: Sword & Sworcery EP features an album's worth of original music by noted Canadian composer Jim Guthrie.

LINELIGHT
iOS, Android

25 *Linelight* is proof that a good game doesn't have to be complicated. The basic idea of the game is that you need to guide a little light along a line. New puzzle mechanics are introduced to test your brain and force you to find clever solutions to continue on your path.

OWLBOY
Nintendo Switch

24 Explore a wondrous world set high up in the clouds in this fantastic 2-D platformer. There are huge dungeons to explore, tough bosses to battle, sky pirates, monsters, and more. You can pick up the friends you meet on the way and fly around with them to use their special abilities.

ALTO'S ODYSSEY iOS

23 A sequel to the critically acclaimed *Alto's Adventure*, *Alto's Odyssey* is a brilliant sandboarding journey through dunes, canyons, and mysterious temples. Simple one-button controls are combined with dynamic lighting and weather effects to create an immersive and beautiful-looking adventure game.

OLD MAN'S JOURNEY
iOS, Android

 22 A game about life's precious moments, broken dreams, and changed plans. You can interact with the environment, squashing and stretching hills to ease the old man's path. It tells a great story, as well as being an incredibly fun puzzle game.

SPLATOON 2
Nintendo Switch

21 *Splatoon 2* is at its best in multiplayer, so if you're lucky enough to have internet wherever it is that you're playing in portable mode, you're going to be able to take that awesome paint-splatting multiplayer experience on the go. If not, *Splatoon 2's* single-player mode is still a lot of fun.

SHOVEL KNIGHT
Nintendo Switch, Nintendo 3DS

 20 Originally released on Nintendo 3DS, *Shovel Knight* recently made its way to the Switch. A fantastic 2-D side-scroller, you play as Shovel Knight as he collects treasure and battles enemies. Switch players can also get their hands on the latest in the series, *King of Cards*.

CASTLE OF ILLUSION
iOS, Android

19 This remake of the classic Sega Genesis game features gorgeous 3-D graphics, as well as all the spookiness of the original. As Mickey Mouse it's your job to rescue Minnie from the titular castle. Each stage has tough jumps, enemies, and puzzles, plus lots of hidden items that unlock new costumes.

MARIO KART 8 DELUXE
Nintendo Switch

18 The Deluxe version of *Mario Kart 8* makes an already great racer even better. It has every track, including the DLC, released for the original Wii U version, and adds new characters like King Boo, Bowser Jr, and the Inklings from *Splatoon*.

SCRIBBLENAUTS UNLIMITED
iOS, Android, Nintendo 3DS

16 A unique platformer, you must use your imagination in *Scribblenauts* to complete a host of tasks. If you can think of something that would solve the problem, type the word, and the object will appear in the game. You can also use adjectives to change existing items. Unlike previous games in the series, which were level-based, *Scribblenauts Unlimited* has an open map you can explore to find cool secrets.

LAYTON'S MYSTERY JOURNEY: KATRIELLE AND THE MILLIONAIRES' CONSPIRACY
iOS, Android, Nintendo 3DS

17 You play as Katrielle, the daughter of the star of the long-running *Layton* series, Professor Layton. Katrielle has opened up a detective agency, so it's your job to solve a series of cases that have proved too tricky for the police. Solving a variety of satisfying puzzles will help to gradually unravel the game's intriguing mystery.

DROPMIX iOS, Android

15 In this cool music-mixing game, you've got to combine cards that represent the different elements from hit songs to create awesome tracks. In Clash Mode, you can go up against a friend to test your mixing skills by meeting the requests as quickly as you can.

SONIC MANIA
Nintendo Switch

14 Sonic is back at his very best in this speedy 2-D platforming masterpiece. You can play as Sonic, Tails, or Knuckles as you race through amazing new zones and remixed classics. Expect plenty of exciting moments, brilliant bosses, and even a few cool surprises along the way.

DID YOU KNOW?
Sonic Mania was nominated for "Best Platformer" and "Best Nintendo Switch Game" at E3 2017, but lost out to *Super Mario Odyssey*.

HEARTHSTONE
iOS, Android

13 After carefully preparing a deck to suit your strategy, playing cards at the right moment, and, finally, defeating your opponent, *Hearthstone* will make you feel like a tactical genius. That's what makes this crafty card game so rewarding. The fact that it is free-to-play makes it even better.

ARMS Nintendo Switch

12 Anyone can jump into *Arms*, start swinging those springy limbs around, and have a lot of fun. What makes the game great, however, is that you discover new layers as you customize your character and start to master its brilliant and bizarre fighting system.

MARIO + RABBIDS: KINGDOM BATTLE
Nintendo Switch

11 The worlds of Mario and the Rabbids collide to create a fresh and funny new experience. Starring Mario, Princess Peach, Luigi, Yoshi, and a rabble of Rabbids dressed up like them, *Kingdom Battle* is a strategic turn-based battle game that is as rewarding as it is hilarious. You can perform up to three actions with each character during your turn. You've got to carefully plan these moves to keep your characters protected behind cover, outmaneuver enemy Rabbids, and take them down with attacks and special abilities.

FORTNITE
iOS

10 It may be hard to believe but *Fortnite* on iPhone and iPad is the same game you get on home consoles. Take on everyone in 100-player battle royales until you're the last player standing. With the mobile version, you and your friends can get together in the same room, start a squad, and then run around the map, gathering equipment, and talking through your plans.

TERRARIA
iOS, Android, Nintendo 3DS, Switch

9 This 2-D sandbox will keep you engrossed for hours. Explore, dig, build, fight, and gather resources to explore further, dig deeper, and build more elaborate structures. With over 100 recipes and more than 300 enemies, each time you load up the game you'll experience something new.

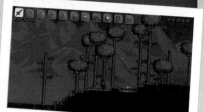

RAYMAN ADVENTURES
Android, iOS

8 A fully-fledged *Rayman* platformer on mobile devices. There are over 50 characters to play as and an impressive 200-plus levels over seven worlds to complete. There is a ton of replayability as each level has a bunch of hidden collectibles for you to find.

MONUMENT VALLEY 2
iOS, Android

7 The original *Monument Valley* is an all-time mobile classic and the follow-up doesn't disappoint. It looks just as beautiful as the first entry and delivers a bunch of amazing new perspective-based puzzles to test your brain power. It's the perfect puzzler for your portable device.

KIRBY: STAR ALLIES
Nintendo Switch

6 The adorable pink blob that is Kirby is known for sucking up enemies to gain their special abilities. You can still do that in *Star Allies*, but Kirby's got another trick up its sleeve. By hitting enemies with hearts, Kirby can get them to join, creating a party of up to four helpers to follow along.

LARA CROFT GO
Android, iOS, PS Vita

5 Unlike the action-adventure games from the *Tomb Raider* series, *Lara Croft GO* is a turn-based puzzle game. You still explore ruins and fight wild animals, but how you go about doing so is completely different. Levels are short and fun, but will keep you engrossed for a long time.

MINECRAFT
Nintendo Switch, iOS, Android, PS Vita

4 There are so many options when it comes to how you play *Minecraft*, but whether you choose the Switch, Vita, or mobile versions, the important thing is that you're getting a great game. The game's unlimited potential for building whatever pops into your imagination keeps it going as strong as ever.

POKÉMON ULTRA SUN & POKÉMON ULTRA MOON
Nintendo 3DS, Nintendo 2DS

3 The *Pokémon* series has long been one of the best in handheld gaming and *Sun* and *Moon* uphold that tradition. The *Ultra* versions improve the base game with the addition of a new Island Trial, a gym-style battle arena, new bosses, and more Pokémon to catch.

SUPER MARIO ODYSSEY **Nintendo Switch**

2 The greatest platformer series of all time delivers again with a fantastic 3-D adventure that you can play on the go. Mario has an awesome new power in *Odyssey*: he can throw his hat-shaped friend, Cappy, to take control of enemies, animals, and objects to help you progress, collect hidden moons, and discover awesome secrets.

THE LEGEND OF ZELDA: BREATH OF THE WILD
Nintendo Switch

1 Who would have thought that you could pack an open world this big, with this much to do, into a portable experience? *Breath of the Wild* is a roaring success in everything it does: open-world exploration, combat, puzzles, exploration, quests, characters, and so on. What really makes it shine is that its open not only in the sense that it takes place in a huge world that you're free to explore at your will, but in that it lets you find creative solutions to the challenges you face. You never know what you might come across next, but you know there will be a million different ways to overcome it—an honestly thrilling combination.

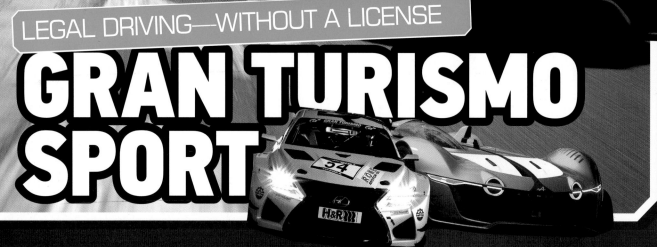

LEGAL DRIVING—WITHOUT A LICENSE

GRAN TURISMO SPORT

Gran Turismo is a series that's been going for over 20 years, so you can be sure its creators know a thing or two about virtual driving simulators. It's unsurprising, then, that *Gran Turismo Sport* is one of the best—and most realistic—racing games ever made.

Rather than going down the path of making you work your way from a battered old wreck up to a glistening supercar, *GT Sport* is about racing through and through. You will start with a vehicle most of us could only dream of owning in real life, and work from there to get better—and faster—automobiles. Racing against the computer, your own times (and ghost cars), or online against real players, there's a huge challenge at all times.

Don't be afraid of the challenge, though—use it to learn, and to help you become one of the best virtual drivers in the world!

STATS

162 cars at launch (with more coming as downloadable content)

2,586 brake horse power for the SRT Tomahawk X Vision Gran Turismo

30 LAPS IN *GT SPORT'S* LONGEST RACE (IT TAKES ABOUT AN HOUR!)

40 layouts of 17 tracks—you've a long way to race

TOP 5 CARS

Cars from different categories that are well worth a ride

DODGE VISION GT

DODGE
SRT TOMAHAWK
VISION GRAN TURISMO TECHNOLOGY

Brand Central

| Displacement | 7000 cc | Max. Power | 2,586 BHP @ 13,800 rpm | Max. Torque | 124.2 kgfm @ 11,300 r |
| Length | --- mm | Width | --- mm | Height | --- m |

DID YOU KNOW?

Gran Turismo creator Kazunori Yamauchi actually became a real-life professional race driver in 2009, driving with Nissan, Lexus, BMW, and more.

SRT TOMAHAWK X VISION GRAN TURISMO

1 The absolute fastest Gr X rank car in the game, the Tomahawk X comes in at over 2,500 horsepower, and can reach speeds of up to 413 miles per hour (665 km/h). You literally cannot beat it on a straight. Two things hold it back: first that it costs a million credits; second that it doesn't (and can't) actually exist in real life.

CHEVROLET CORVETTE STINGRAY

2 Located in the N500 ranks, this lovely Corvette struggles with corners and braking, but at 51,000 credits and with a huge top speed for the price, you'll have got a bargain if you control it in the bends.

| cc Max. Power | 389 BHP @ 7,000 rpm | Max. Torque | 47.2 kgfm @ 4,000 rpm |
| Width | 1,812 mm | Height | 1,427 mm |

MITSUBISHI LANCER EVOLUTION FINAL EDITION

3 The Gr.4 ranked Evo Final Edition is a great car at a good price, but it's also the last time Mitsubishi will be making this model.

BUGATTI VEYRON 16.4 2013

4 Located in the N1000 rank, the Veyron is a modern-day legend. You'll need to learn to handle it on the corners, but this beast is one of the fastest cars in the world.

AUDI QUATTRO S1 PIKES PEAK 1987

5 Finishing with a Gr B rank is the classic Audi Quattro. On a race track there's plenty that will leave it behind, but on dirt and snow there are few better cars in the world.

TIPS & TRICKS

Practice in Circuit Experience
Not only does Circuit Experience teach you the tracks (and cars), but it also gives a nice payout of both credits and XP.

Follow the racing line
See the darker area of the track, where lots of tyres have been before? That's the racing line. Stick to it!

Try lots of cars
You might find a car you like, but you won't find one you really love until you experiment with everything *GT Sport* has to offer.

Tuning
It's tricky, but with time you will be pushing your cars beyond their stock performance and into tuned-up glory.

Customise your car
This doesn't help you win races, but putting unique decals on your car helps you stand out from the crowd—and look cool!

POKÉMON ULTRA SUN & ULTRA MOON

A LEGENDARY RETURN TO ALOLA

With their tropical setting, variety of game modes, and fresh new takes on fan-favorite monsters, *Pokémon Sun and Moon* instantly became some of the most popular titles in the long-running series. Now trainers can embark on a brand-new *Pokémon* adventure in *Ultra Sun* and *Ultra Moon*. You'll still be catching, training, and battling a team of monsters to beat rival trainers and complete island trials, but you'll also travel to new worlds filled with legendary Pokémon through Ultra Wormholes. Not to mention unraveling the mystery of the Necrozma . . .

Whether this is your first trip to Alola or you're a returning Pokémon master looking to add legendary power to your team, *Ultra Sun* and *Ultra Moon* have plenty to keep you entertained.

STATS

84
METACRITIC SCORE FOR ULTRA SUN & ULTRA MOON

807
total number of known Pokémon

100
Zygarde cores needed to assemble its true form

15.91 MILLION
copies of *Pokémon Sun* and *Moon* sold

TOP 5 LEGENDARY POKÉMON
Iconic characters from the franchise

Mewtwo

1 It's been years since Mewtwo was introduced as one of the very first legendary Pokémon, but the powerful Psychic-type still ranks as one of the best. Available to catch by traveling to an alternate dimension, it's a powerful ally to have. Making use of its two mega evolutions can boost its frightening power even further.

Suicune

2 The cover star of *Pokémon Crystal* remains one of the most iconic legendary Pokémon around, with a moveset including Blizzard and Hydro Pump making it a real special attack powerhouse. Living up to its elusive reputation, Suicune won't appear unless you're carrying both Entei and Raikou in your party.

Rayquaza

3 Rayquaza is famously the legendary Pokémon meant to keep Groudon and Kyogre in check, so it's fitting that you'll need both those monsters in your team before you can encounter the fearsome Dragon/ Flying-type. Not only is it spectacularly powerful, it's also a gigantic dragon. Just look at it—it's awesome!

Xerneas

4 A lot of the most powerful Pokémon around are Dragon- type, but Xerneas can wipe the floor with them. Its Fairy typing means it stays immune from Dragon attacks, while punishing them with a powerful Moonblast itself. It's exclusive to *Ultra Sun*, so if you're an *Ultra Moon* player you'll have to find someone to trade with.

Kyurem

5 Already a powerful all-rounder, this Pokémon's dual typing helps negate a key weakness to ice-type moves. But Kyurem's real potential is only revealed when it's combined with either Zekrom or Reshiram. The resulting Black and White variations are truly a force to be reckoned with.

TIPS & TRICKS

Chat to Rotom
Don't ignore Rotom, your trusty talking Pokédex, when it tries to talk to you. Being nice to it nets a serious reward.

Photo friends
Taking photos of your Pokémon for the Alola Photo Club can help in unexpected ways, like boosting the amount of EXP they gain.

No boys allowed
If you're wondering why your Salandit won't evolve into a Salazzle, check its gender. Only female Salandits can evolve!

Surf's up!
The new Mantine Surf mini-game is a fast way to travel between islands, but it's also good for racking up Battle Points.

Seek out stickers
Look out for Totem Stickers littered about Alola. Trading these in to Samson Oak can net you some powerful Totem Pokémon.

MEET THE SUPERFAN

FAMILIAR FOES

Archie

Team Aqua's vaguely pirate-like boss once aimed to use legendary Pokémon Kyogre to expand the oceans, so he should be right at home on the wide open seas of Alola.

Lysandre

Last seen trying to eradicate almost all human life in *Pokémon X* and *Y*, the leader of Team Flare is back. We hope he's mellowed out a bit, but we wouldn't count on it.

LISA COURTNEY

Who?

Lisa Courtney isn't just any *Pokémon* superfan. Her massive collection of *Pokémon* toys, games, and many other kinds of merchandise has been verified as the largest in the world by Guinness World Records—and it's still growing! At the last count, Lisa's collection numbered over 17,000 items.

Why?

Quite simply, Lisa loves *Pokémon* in all of its many different forms, whether it's the games, the TV series, comic books, or plush toys. And while she's not sure that she will ever be able to "catch 'em all," Lisa says that nothing beats the thrill of a new *Pokémon*-themed item arriving in the post.

ALSO CHECK OUT . . .

Yo-kai Watch 2

The massively popular *Yo-kai Watch* series borrows several elements from *Pokémon*, but it's still a really great adventure that is built around discovering and collecting loads of different creatures before leading them into battle with others.

DID YOU KNOW?

The opening area of Melemele Island is based on the real-life Hawaiian island of Oahu, with Hau'oli City standing in for Honolulu.

THE EXPERT SAYS...
SHIGERU OHMORI

Directing *Pokémon Sun and Moon*, producing *Pokémon Ultra Sun* and *Ultra Moon*

In an interview with *games™* Shigeru Ohmori said, "I really wanted to make a fun, new-feeling game. We went in and tweaked various little bits—the thought process was to rethink everything *Pokémon* was about and if we could change areas of the game, we would try to. We tried various things and settled on a few, like changing the Gyms, for example. This is a new approach for *Pokémon* and by doing this, we're able to get a really fresh feel for both new players and those that have been playing for a long time."

Giovanni

The head of the infamous Team Rocket and original bad guy from *Pokémon Red* and *Blue* has once again reared his head to cause trouble—this time in Alola.

Ghetsis

The boss of Team Plasma returns after being introduced in *Pokémon Black* and *White*. Despite a humbling defeat, he's still up to his old tricks. And his dress sense doesn't seem to have improved either.

Monster Hunter Stories

This spin-off game puts you in the role of a hero who can hatch, raise, and ride a variety of fearsome monsters. Great customization options let you make your beasts truly unique.

Xenoblade Chronicles 2

In size and length, *Xenoblade Chronicles 2* dwarfs even *Pokémon Ultra Sun* and *Ultra Moon*, but for anyone who really wants a meaty RPG to sink their teeth into, it's an easy game to recommend.

DID YOU KNOW?

The very first version of *Minecraft* was created in just six days, before it was released into Early Access on PC.

UP ALL NIGHT TO GET CRAFTY

MINECRAFT

Everybody loves *Minecraft*—Mojang's **masterpiece that lets players express their creativity or explore unmapped worlds in survival.** Want to build a house? You can do that. Want to venture out into the darkness of night in search of gleaming treasure? You can do that. Want to build a working in-game calculator? It would be rather time consuming and difficult, but yeah, you can do that, too!

Minecraft is a game that never ends. While there is always something to build, thanks to the game's randomly generated terrains, you'll never run out of new worlds to explore.

This never-ending game continues to receive free updates, and with the introduction of the Better Together Update, there has never been a better time to pick up your pickaxe and get crafting.

STATS

MINECRAFT HAS SOLD OVER

122
MILLION COPIES

Since launch, *Minecraft* has sold an average of around **55,000 COPIES PER DAY**

AROUND
55 million
crafters play *Minecraft* each month

If everyone who played *Minecraft* each month were to hold hands, they'd fit around the entire planet

FUN FOR ALL

PLAY WITH ANYONE

There has never been a better time to play *Minecraft* with a bunch of friends. With the release of the Better Together Update, players on Xbox One, Mobile, and Nintendo Switch, can all play together in the same world regardless of what platform they're on.

BUILD LITERALLY ANYTHING

It goes without saying, *Minecraft* will always be about building. Whatever you can imagine, you can build it. From small, dirt huts to pixel art; from towering skyscrapers to complex redstone, *Minecraft* lets us create anything. And with seemingly endless possibilities, the sky's the limit for what we can accomplish.

NEW AREAS

Have you visited one of the latest new zones, the End City, yet? After you've defeated the dreaded Ender Dragon, head back to the area, search, and you'll find a collection of bedrocks with a portal inside. Throw an ender pearl into the portal, and you'll be transported to a new area.

STORY CONTENT

Despite the release of Telltale's excellent point-and-click adventure *Minecraft: Story Mode*, the original *Minecraft* is missing a campaign mode of its own. Fortunately, the new Marketplace offers exciting adventure map packs—featuring new mobs, new worlds, and new gameplay—for every occasion.

ALSO CHECK OUT . . .

Terraria

What happens when you take *Minecraft* and make it 2-D? You get *Terraria*. Designed with that 8-bit feel you know and love, *Terraria* lets players craft, survive, and explore just like in *Minecraft*, only on a flat screen.

Dragon Quest Builders

With lovely graphics and an anime feel, *Dragon Quest Builders* lets you build your home, round up characters to help you, and defend your town against monsters. It's even got its own Story mode.

DID YOU KNOW?

Unlike most games, everything in *Cuphead* is drawn by hand, like an old cartoon. That includes all of the backgrounds, bosses and animations!

DON'T BE A MUG

CUPHEAD

Cuphead **might look like a lovely little adventure, but you should never judge a game by its graphics.** Inspired by classic run-and-gun action games like *Contra* and *Gunstar Heroes*, *Cuphead* delights in putting you in front of a relentless onslaught of crazy bosses—some of whom are so big that they hardly fit on the screen! Those classic cartoon graphics hide a super-challenging game.

We won't lie to you, *Cuphead* is really, really hard, but it's also a lot of fun. It's got a unique visual style, an amazing soundtrack, and some of the most interesting boss battles in gaming—you'll just need to put in the time to see them all. Practice makes perfect, and it rewards those with patience; if you're looking for something to hone your gaming skills you'll want to get involved with this wonderfully tough action game.

STATS

1930s
the decade of animation that inspired *Cuphead*'s visual style and design

TWO-PLAYER CO-OP ACTION

There are
19
unique bosses

3
WORLDS TO PLAY THROUGH

TOP 5 TOUGHEST BOSSES

Show off your skills by besting these difficult baddies

GRIM MATCHSTICK

1 If any boss is going to cause you difficulties in *Cuphead* it's going to be Inkwell Isle II's Grim Matchstick. You'll need deft platforming skills and pixel perfect precision with your bullets to make it through this encounter alive; this three-headed dragon might look awesome, but it's a nightmare to best!

DR. KAHL'S ROBOT

2 Make it through Dr. Kahl's Robot battle and you'll earn some mad respect from us. This boss has one of the hardest phases to conquer in the game; the last segment of this battle will test your controller skills and patience.

BEPPI THE CLOWN

3 Beppi is the first difficulty wall you'll hit in the game. It's a long battle that will require a lot of studying to make it through alive; keep your eyes on the bottom and corners of the screen as this battle is full of environmental dangers.

CALA MARIA

4 Cala Maria has an attack that will paralyze poor Cuphead and Mugman in place for a few seconds, making it impossible to dodge the volleys of projectiles constantly streaming towards you. Take it one phase at a time and try to stay calm and collected while you do it.

KING DICE

5 Hit the casino and you'll be nearing the end of the game, close to confronting the Devil. But to do that you'll first need to get past King Dice, and he's a total nightmare! You'll need mad parrying skills to make it off the table and into an audience with the evil overlord.

TIPS & TRICKS

Bring a friend
Cuphead supports two player co-op. Bring a friend and they can pull you back into the fight after you lose all of your HP.

Practice hard!
This game is supposed to be difficult, but it isn't impossible! Keep going and you'll get through all those bosses eventually.

Don't rush it
It can be easy to get frustrated and rush into boss encounters, but you need to stay patient and wait for openings before attacking them.

Pay attention
The bosses have a set pattern that you can learn. Pay attention and it'll help you dodge all of the projectiles coming your way.

Three phases
The bosses each have three phases, changing up their attack pattern after you inflict a certain amount of damage. Watch out for these!

NOT SO FINAL AFTER ALL

FINAL FANTASY SERIES

The *Final Fantasy* series started in 1987 on the NES, and has continued to grow and expand, bringing in new fans and introducing countless people to RPGs (and games as a whole) to this day. The most recent release in the main series, *Final Fantasy XV*, is available on PS4, Xbox One, and PC and has proved just as popular among fans as the original game, proving this is a series with a dedicated, loving fanbase who will support it . . . well, forever. All of the main games tell a different, unconnected story (though there are spin-offs and tie-ins), but all contain similar game mechanics like leveling up, using different items and a few repeating characters, or at least names. And now PS4 owners will be able to experience arguably the greatest game in the series with *Final Fantasy VII Remake* coming to the console.

STATS

OVER 130 MILLION copies have been sold

54 titles have been released over 30 years

$137 million budget for *Final Fantasy: The Spirits Within* movie

1997 the first time a main *Final Fantasy* game was released outside of Japan and the US

TOP 5 HEROES

The coolest characters in the *Final Fantasy* world

Cloud

1 Cloud is a typical *Final Fantasy* hero, but he's remained a favorite with fans for more than 20 years now. Quiet and calm, powerful in battle, and able to take on entire armies by himself, there's a special place in a lot of hearts for the guy with the huge sword and the silly hair.

Steiner

2 Zidane is cool, and Princess Garnet goes on an emotional rollercoaster—and special mention for Vivi here—but we can't get past how great Steiner is. A bumbling idiot turns into a genuine hero, grows as a man, and learns that there's more to life than just serving the crown.

Lightning

3 She might not smile very much, but who can blame her with the challenges Lightning has to face throughout her adventures. But there's no doubting she's also one of the strongest and coolest *Final Fantasy* protagonists we've ever played as in any of the games.

Balthier

4 While *Final Fantasy XII* might be about Vaan, really the character to pay attention to is Balthier. He's cool, cocky, and suave, and his friend Fran is just as cool as the man himself. How could she not be when she's a seven-foot-tall rabbit person?

Yuna

5 Yuna is a summoner struggling with her place in the world in *Final Fantasy X*. By the time *X-2* comes around she's in a group of strong-minded friends who go around the world solving problems, making her one of the series' most impressive heroines. And she's in a band!

TIPS & TRICKS

Grind
Less so in the newer games, but in older *FF* games you do have to fight weaker enemies a lot to level up. But it's well worth it.

Change characters
When you're sticking with one party, the rest of your characters aren't leveling up, so the grind isn't working on them. Switch them out!

Use your summons
Not every game has them, but when you can use summons you should—dragons always help!

Don't ignore the old games
As well as teaching you about the series, the original *FF* titles teach you a lot about games themselves. They're living museum pieces!

Replay Final Fantasy VII
Don't just play through the best *FF* once—return to this classic with the upcoming PS4 remake, too.

THE DEV SPEAKS

BEST GAMES

Final Fantasy VII
The one everyone talks about, and with good reason—*Final Fantasy VII* introduced a whole generation to the world of Japanese RPGs. It's still brilliant, and there's now an awesome new remake coming to PS4.

Final Fantasy XV
The latest in the main series is a bold step, changing things up a lot and mixing up the classic formula. It could have gone wrong . . . but it didn't! *Final Fantasy XV* is great for newcomers and veterans alike.

HAJIME TABATA

Who?
Hajime Tabata has worked on a number of games in the *Final Fantasy* series and took on the role of director for *Final Fantasy XV*.

On his inspirations for *FFXV*...
"I [had] a lot of inspiration from almost all open-world games coming from the Western game market these days, of course. However, the actual inspiration for having a seamless world in *Final Fantasy XV*—that you can travel through without any breaks—came from, funnily enough, *The Legend of Zelda: Ocarina of Time* on Nintendo 64. That was my biggest inspiration for that idea."

ALSO CHECK OUT . . .

Kingdom Hearts series
If you took *Final Fantasy* and mixed it with Disney, what would happen? Why, the *Kingdom Hearts* series, of course! All of the games are worth playing, with players battling alongside Goofy, Donald Duck, and other characters.

DID YOU KNOW?

Every main *FF* game after the first features a character called Cid, and they're always an engineer, linked to an airship, or both!

THE EXPERT SAYS . . .
HOLLIE BENNETT
PlayStation Access

The *Final Fantasy* series isn't just another collection of games; it's a collection of games that fueled a lifelong passion which even pushed me into pursuing a career in the industry. As a kid from a small town in rural South Wales the *Final Fantasy* series fed my imagination like nothing else, taking me to exotic worlds and on epic adventures, something I could never dream of doing. I fell in love with the characters, listened endlessly to the music, and daydreamed about their epic stories. Even as I sit here typing this, wearing a Cactuar necklace and listening to a Discord channel full of friends I've made through a mutual love of *Final Fantasy*, I can honestly say no other game series has had such a meaningful and lasting impact on me like *Final Fantasy* has.

> WEDGE: Not to worry. The Sla Crown on her head robs her all conscious thought. She'll
> orders.

Final Fantasy VI

If you want the best example of the "classic" *Final Fantasy* games, look no further than number six. You can play this brilliant retro title on the SNES Mini, so look out for it there.

Final Fantasy XII

Originally on PS2—later on PS4 —*FFXII* is an overlooked gem in the series, offering unique play and a bunch of brilliant characters that it's worth playing just to get to know.

Undertale

A love letter to RPGs like *Final Fantasy*, *Undertale* pokes fun at its inspirations as much as it pays homage to them. It's warm, funny, and short enough that it doesn't take too long to finish!

Secret of Mana

You can get this great RPG on the SNES Mini—it's action and timing-based rather than fought in turns, so it's more demanding on your reactions. It's also, even decades after its first release, brilliant fun.

DID YOU SEE THAT?!

FINAL FANTASY XV

Final Fantasy XV **has everything a great RPG should: a vast world to explore, great characters, and memorable moments.** One of the highlights that got fans of the series excited was the quest to get the Chocobo Whistle. Chocobos have been a part of *Final Fantasy* since 1988 and in the latest game, Noctis and his party can call upon the animal at any time for a ride, but only if they help out at the Chocobo Post . . .

1 When Noctis and his friends arrive at the Wiz Chocobo Post, the owner tells them that the animals have to stay inside as a behemoth named Deadeye is roaming and the birds are too scared to leave. If they want to ride the Chocobos, they will need to take care of Deadeye.

2 After exploring the rocky hillside, the group discover a concrete wall with a small hole in the corner that's just big enough to crawl through. Crawling through the tight passageway, they come across Deadeye, unaware that he is being stalked. Staying quiet is a definite must.

3 The group decides that the best place to surprise Deadeye is in his lair, so they follow him until he goes back to rest. The party stays back, sticking to the rocks and trees, keeping their distance from Deadeye and out of his sight. Thankfully, the mist helps the group stay hidden.

4 Eventually the party finds Deadeye in the ruins of an abandoned factory. Using fire magic and the explosive barrels, the guys take down the beast. They return to the Chocobo Post to collect their reward. Now the party can freely roam on the back of a Chocobo whenever they want.

DID YOU KNOW?

Some reviewers described *Destiny 2* as "Destiny 1.5" due to its similarities to the original, yet it averaged an impressive 85 on Metacritic.

DESTINY 2

TRAVELER'S TALES

Return to the world of Guardians, Ghaul, and Golden Exotics in Bungie's explosive sequel. If you're a fan of the original, then you've no doubt already sunk your teeth deep into *Destiny 2*'s story; if you're just passing by and are interested, however, you've got a lot to get excited about. Excellent combat, a deep leveling system, and a host of different gameplay modes for both Player versus Player and Player versus Environment await you. *Destiny 2* is bigger, louder, and overall a more mature game than the original. In this sequel you'll be sticking it to the monstrous Cabal in order to save the mysterious Traveler. Oh, and you'll be doing a lot of that "save the planet from exploding" thing, which is pretty popular these days. What lies beyond that . . . well, that'd be telling. You'll have to dive in and find out for yourself.

STATS

33% **33%** **33%** Equal amounts of players choose to main each class: that's impressive!

Destiny 2 was the 2nd **BIGGEST SELLING** console game of 2017

89.7% PLAYERS USED PROMETHEUS LENS ON "TRIALS OF OSIRIS" RELEASE WEEK

OVER 1.25 billion enemies have been killed by Guardians firing off their Super

TOP 5 WEIRD WEAPONS

The weird and wonderful gear in *Destiny 2*

WARDCLIFF COIL

1 This is a . . . uh, small satellite? A disco ball? Or is it just a heap of junk that's haphazardly thrown together? Whatever, it doesn't matter. This rocket launcher fires off a flurry of rockets that home in on your enemies. It also reloads itself when holstered, what more could you want?

PROMETHEUS LENS

2 When this crystal-powered weapon dropped with the "Trials of Osiris" expansion it was broken—and we mean "broken" in the "Oh my, this is so powerful. How did Bungie let this happen?!" way. It sends out a super-hot beam of energy that disintegrates pretty much anything. It's hotter than your favorite hot sauce.

TRACTOR CANNON

4 We'll level with you: this Shotgun is pretty useless unless you want to eliminate an enemy by catapulting them off a cliff. It sends a shockwave out, which doesn't do a lot of damage, yet has a lot of power behind it. A curio, for sure, and something you use if you're into showboating.

TELESTO

3 Ah, Telesto, the besto. It's a unique fusion rifle that fires off glowing purple globs that stick to enemies. "What, that's all?" we imagine you're saying. Well, no. The globs explode in pretty purple explosions, which then reload the gun on multikills. It's basically essential for any wannabe space-warrior princess.

SUNSHOT

5 Hand Cannons are cool and all, but what about one that harnesses the power of the Sun? Yeah: awesome, right? The Sunshot can make enemies explode, making it one of the more useful Energy weapons in the game. It also reloads by slotting weird spheres into its chamber.

ALSO CHECK OUT . . .

Halo 5: Guardians
Way before *Destiny* was a thing, Bungie was making *Halo*. As Master Chief, the latest game in the series lets you command a group of Spartans while you fight the mysterious enemy threatening to destroy the galaxy.

Overwatch
You think you're king of the Crucible and want to take it to the next level, gear up, and hit up the best competitive FPS this generation. Just remember: you need to play the objective in this one, so you'll need to think about what you're doing.

ORI AND THE WILL OF THE WISPS

A NEW LIGHT EMERGES FROM THE DARK

Ori and the Blind Forest **was special.** It was beautiful, expansive, and challenging—a real surprise when it launched in 2015 for Xbox One and PC. Thankfully, developer Moon Studios is giving us another opportunity to drop into this stunning world as guardian spirit Ori. In this side-scrolling platformer it's up to you to use your intuition, pixel-perfect jumps, and puzzle-solving abilities to navigate and survive a gorgeous world fraught with danger. Extending beyond the forest setting of the original game, *Ori and the Will of the Wisps* is a huge expansion to its predecessor, introducing all-new abilities, new upgrade systems, and fresh ways to use your range of powers. Expect to encounter some real challenges on this journey, but if you can overcome it you'll find something truly impressive waiting.

STATS

2,000
Number of iterations the **reveal trailer** went through before being released

1,100,000 VIEWS of the reveal trailer on **YouTube**

11 SKILLS to learn as Ori *ori*

1 new world to explore

TOP 5 CHARACTERS

Get caught up with Ori's story

THE SPIRIT TREE

2 The guardian of the forest of Nibel, the Spirit Tree possesses a variety of powers that it uses to help keep the area safe from harm. The mystical being is the creator of protagonist Ori and is charged with sending you off on adventure anew.

SEIN

4 Ori's companion throughout these troubled lands, Sein is a creature that contains the power of the Spirit Tree, acting as both your ward and weapon throughout the adventure. Sein can be upgraded with ability points to increase its power in combat, and gain new abilities.

ORI

1 The game's titular character and starring protagonist, Ori is a spirit guardian that finds itself in the unlikely position of forest savior—helping to restore the spirit tree and quell the flames raining down from Mount Horu. This new adventure is Ori's most challenging yet.

KURO'S CHILD

3 While the fearsome owl Kuro perished in *Ori and the Blind Forest*, we haven't seen the last of it. After Kuro's egg was rescued by Naru, the last of the owl hatchlings could become an unlikely ally to Ori.

NARU

5 Naru is a powerful figure in *Ori and the Blind Forest*, acting as a surrogate parent for Ori and, spoilers, eventual savior. Naru, and her newfound friend Gumo, watch on with pride in what Ori had accomplished, but you just know they will be along for the ride when adventure calls.

TIPS & TRICKS

Investigate everything
The game is packed with collectibles and secret areas to uncover, so be sure to investigate every area fully before moving on.

Save all the time
Ori and the Will of the Wisps is a real challenge, filled with tricky areas, so don't be afraid to spend your cache of blue orbs to save the game frequently.

Be aware
If you're struggling to make it through an area, double-check that you don't have ability points to spend on unlocking new upgrades.

Be agile
A platformer at heart, you'll need to use meticulous timing with your jumps to avoid enemies and hazards in the environment.

Don't give up
If you find yourself at a loss, try returning to a previous area of the game and see if your upgraded abilities have unlocked new areas of play.

FORZA MOTORSPORT 7

FEEL THE SPEED!

If you like the sound of roaring around a track at high speed in the fastest and coolest cars in the world, then *Forza Motorsport* **is the game for you.** The latest entry brings more cars than ever before in a *Forza* game, as well as a new track, and hundreds of events to take part in. Plus, the new dynamic weather system can change a race completely—if it starts raining, you'll need to take more care as you try to take tight corners in case you skid off the track!

The game looks awesome no matter how you play, but it also supports 4K and HDR for even better graphics. If you are playing on an Xbox One X and have a 4K TV it might trick you into thinking you really are driving around at 200mph in a brand-new Porsche.

STATS

722 cars at launch

14 million registered players

269 mph fastest recorded speed

200+ **unique** track configurations

TOP 5 COOLEST CARS
Looking good and driving fast!

PORSCHE 911 GT2 RS

1 The latest car from Porsche can do 0-62mph in an impressive 2.8 seconds, and with a top speed of 211mph it's no slouch in the straights. When you hit the accelerate button on your controller, you'll seriously feel the rumble of the powerful engine under your finger.

RENAULT R.S.17

2 This Formula 1 car is a digital recreation of the one that Nico Hülkenberg drove in the 2017 F1 season. As one of the fastest cars in the game, this is the vehicle you'll use to set the very fastest lap times. The pure speed makes playing in cockpit view thrilling.

FORD GT FORZA EDITION

3 The 2015 Ford GT was the cover star of the last *Motorsport* title, and this special version of the 2017 model is one of the coolest cars to drive in *Forza 7*. It's a special, finely tuned digital version of the supercar, meaning this game is the only way to actually experience how it feels.

MERCEDES-AMG GT S

4 This special car is part of the *Fate of the Furious* movie DLC, which makes it a one-of-a-kind vehicle. Just like in the movie, you might find that this car skids around a little, but that just means you'll need to use your drifting skills to get it back under control.

FERRARI FXX K

5 The "K" in this hypercar's name represents the kinetic energy recovery system, or KERS, which allows it to boost the power of the engine. The result is a car with 1,036 horsepower and a top speed of 214mph. Two mini spoilers help the car get more grip and also look incredibly cool.

TIPS & TRICKS

Weather-ready
Be prepared for the weather to change mid-race and adjust your driving style. If it starts raining, you'll need to brake earlier!

Turn on assists
You can choose whether driving assists (like auto-braking) are enabled or not, but there is no disadvantage to having them switched on.

Brake straight
When approaching a corner, braking when your wheels are pointing straight forward will help you slow down quicker and turn more tightly!

Next step
It's tough to master, but if you want to get faster times, changing your gearbox to manual can help you shave seconds off your laps.

Wheeler dealer
In the Car tab of the main menu, keep checking on the Speciality Dealer. Here you can buy rare cars, with stock that changes regularly.

TOP 🔟 GAMING Y▶UTUBERS

Trump

4 YouTube is full of great *Hearthstone* players, but Twitch streamer Trump is one of the very best. His videos are not only fun; they're also informative, as he explains each one of his decisions before making them, offers alternatives he could have made, and regularly posts videos explaining how new cards work. His channel is ideal if you want to get into the game, or just want to improve your *Hearthstone* skills.

CaptainSparklez

5 Another YouTuber specializing in *Minecraft* videos, CaptainSparklez manages to set himself apart from the crowd with his delightful and quirky approach to the game. From attempting tricky challenges to creating full *Minecraft* music videos, the sheer variety of content that the American star manages to create is spectacular. There aren't just gameplay videos either—he's even produced a series of original animated shorts based around the game!

Mark Brown

2 Have you ever wondered what makes Mario's jump feel just right? Or how the devious puzzles in *Zelda* dungeons fit together? Mark Brown's YouTube channel, Game Maker's Toolkit, lets you in on some of the design secrets behind these games and more. If you're curious about how games work then it's a great watch—it could even make you see your favorite game in a whole new light.

Cap Jump

Press and hold ❶ then step on the cap.

DanTDM

1 With over 17 million subscribers and more than 11 billion views across his channel, DanTDM is YouTube royalty. The British star made his name producing brilliant *Minecraft* videos, but he's applied his infectious personality and hilarious sense of humor to plenty of other games as well. Whether you're a huge *Minecraft* fan, or just want to laugh along with Dan and his fantastic comic creations, you'll find loads to enjoy here.

JarradHD

3 Australian YouTuber JarradHD is a must-follow for any *FIFA* fans out there. His videos focus on the game's career mode, and his signature 'Rebuild' series sees him attempt to manage a team from somewhere in the world of soccer to championship glory. JarradHD takes requests on which teams to rebuild too, so make sure to comment if you want to see your favorite side lift the Champions League trophy.

aarava

6 When it comes to racing games, aarava is one of the most prolific YouTubers out there, having racked up over 60 million views playing games like *The Crew 2*, *Forza Motorsport 7*, and *GT Sport*. Make sure to check out his "Survive" series, where he takes on some of the hardest races in *F1 2017* with the Extreme Damage mod enabled. Spoilers: it usually doesn't end well . . .

The Game Theorists

7 This hugely popular channel run by influential YouTuber Matpat is all about game theories. In-depth videos exploring game lore: check. Famous myths busted: absolutely. Wild speculation based on minimal evidence: you bet. The Game Theorists are the first to admit that they're "overanalyzing" everything, but you never know, even the craziest theory might just turn out to be true . . .

Bajan Canadian

8 The beauty of *Minecraft* is that it caters to all sorts of players, and YouTuber Mitch Hughes, better known as Bajan Canadian, is definitely one to watch if you like your *Minecraft* fast, frantic, and fiercely competitive. His combination of unbelievable skills and hilarious commentary has seen him amass almost 2 billion views—mostly by defeating opponents in Survival Games and pulling off crazy jumps in parkour races.

THE EXPERT SAYS . . .
MARK BROWN
Game Maker's Toolkit YouTube channel

I always start a new video with a question for myself, such as "how are levels made in *Mario*?" I then try to find the answer by doing some research, talking to developers, closely analyzing games, and arguing with friends.

The video itself is an opportunity to share what I've learned with others. Some people assume I just know loads about game design, but—unfortunately—that's not true!

In reality I'm just very interested in the way games work, and I've found that creating YouTube videos is a great way to satisfy that curiosity.

Stampylonghead

9 He might have dabbled in a variety of other games, but Stampy will always be known for his *Minecraft* videos, starring his very own creation, Mr. Stampy Cat. Mr. Stampy Cat's zany adventures have seen him gain a loyal following of over 8 million subscribers, and the character was even introduced in *Minecraft: Story Mode*—with Stampy himself providing the voiceover!

Noclip

10 Noclip are a team that specialize in making documentaries on popular games and the people that make them. Their videos are slick and fascinating, and reveal some really interesting stories about how some of the biggest gaming hits of recent times came to be. Their two-part video on the making of *Rocket League* is a great place to start.

▶ 6 TIPS FOR YOUTUBE VIEWING
What you need to know for the best YouTube experience

1 GET AN ACCOUNT
Creating an account doesn't take long and will allow you to subscribe to your favorite channels. When you've subscribed you can find out when they release new videos or go live.

2 VIDEO QUALITY
The video quality is set to Auto by default. To get the best video, click on the gear icon in the bottom-right corner of the screen to set it to Full HD.

3 RECOMMENDED VIDEO
As you watch, subscribe, and like videos, your homepage will have recommended content. Scroll through the homepage to find new channels that relate to what you watch.

4 UNWANTED VIDEOS
If you find an inappropriate video, report it—you'll be helping the YouTube community. You can also mark recommended videos as unwanted to stop them appearing in your feed.

5 PRIVACY SETTINGS
To prevent others from seeing what you like and save on YouTube, go into your Account Settings and select Privacy from the menu along the left-hand side of the screen.

6 RESTRICTED MODE
While on the Settings page, at the bottom of the screen is the option to enable Restricted Mode. This will automatically block any content that has been flagged as being inappropriate.

DID YOU KNOW?

Metroid Prime: Federation Force is heavily inspired by Metroid Prime Hunters, which was released on Nintendo DS in 2006.

METROID

THE CONTINUING ADVENTURES OF SAMUS ARAN

Metroid **might not be as big a Nintendo franchise as** Mario **or** Zelda, **but that doesn't mean it should be ignored.** In fact, there are a variety of fun games available that cover several different genres.

The biggest change for the series takes the form of Metroid Prime: Federation Force, as it allows you to play as a marine of the Galactic Federation for the first time. While it has lots of cool shooting mechanics, it also lets you play Blast Ball—a fun, futuristic sports game that has shades of Rocket League to it.

This is a more traditional Metroid game that has Samus Aran attempting to kill 40 rogue Metroids. It's actually a remake of an old Game Boy game, but has been completely overhauled and has lots of cool new features. It's the perfect game to play while you wait for Metroid Prime 4.

STATS

THE METROID FRANCHISE BEGAN IN **1986**

Metroid was rebooted in **2002** in the form of Metroid Prime

Over **17** MILLION Metroid games have been sold

14 Metroid games have been released so far

TOP 5 METROID GAMES

The best adventures of Samus Aran

ENERGY 99

SUPER METROID

1 This is widely regarded as one of Samus Aran's best adventures and is amazingly atmospheric with lots of memorable boss encounters that will really challenge you. It's also easily available on numerous Nintendo systems, as well as the SNES Mini, so there's no excuse not to play it.

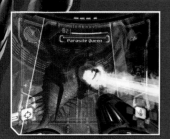

METROID PRIME

2 The first *Metroid Prime* game might look like a first-person shooter, but don't let that put you off. It's still the same old *Metroid* adventure, transporting the action to the third dimension and adding some truly beautiful-looking locations to explore.

METROID FUSION

3 This excellent 2-D adventure was first released for the Game Boy Advance in 2002. It's notable for featuring a deadly clone of Samus that hunts her down during certain parts of the game, making her have to run away. You can also play it on Wii U.

METROID OTHER M

4 Ignore all the drama in the cutscenes and focus on the incredible action. While mostly in third-person, pointing the remote at the screen activates a cool first-person shooting mode that makes it nice and easy to destroy enemies.

METROID PRIME 3: CORRUPTION

5 The third *Prime* game was originally released on Nintendo Wii and makes great use of motion controls. It also adds a Hypermode ability that drains Samus's health but makes her invulnerable.

ALSO CHECK OUT . . .

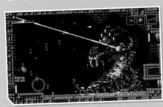

Axiom Verge

This impressive *Metroid* clone is pretty much the sole work of Thomas Happ. It has a style that's very similar to the original NES game and has great bosses to battle. It's available on virtually every current system.

SteamWorld Dig

This is another excellent *Metroid*-inspired game that features a robot who is looking for treasure underneath an old mining town. There's a good story to uncover, different environments, and lots of cool weapons to unlock.

SUPER MARIO ODYSSEY

MARIO'S GREATEST ADVENTURE YET

There's a reason *Super Mario Odyssey* has a Metacritic rating of 97%—it's one of the finest platformers ever made. Full of imagination, and not afraid to push expectations, *Super Mario Odyssey* is a bold, exciting platformer that introduces many new ideas to the *Mario* series, but still ensures it remains familiar to anyone who has loved previous games.

The thing that makes *Super Mario Odyssey* so much fun to play is that Mario's new friend, Cappy, allows him to possess all sorts of enemies in the game, from goombas to dinosaurs, which greatly impacts on how he tackles each stage. It's an astonishing adventure that's filled with wonderful touches to the series, and will take an age to fully complete. A true gaming masterpiece.

STATS

Mario encounters **5 NEW BOSSES** called the Broodals

There are **17** gigantic worlds to discover

Mario can buy and wear **37 DIFFERENT OUTFITS**

There are **7** wedding items to find

TOP 5 THINGS TO POSSESS

There is such a variety of things you can possess!

T-Rex

1 Jumping into this gigantic dinosaur is tremendous fun, as it allows Mario to break up boulders and cause all sorts of damage to his environment. Just remember that it does put a big strain on Cappy's possession powers, meaning he can only possess the dino for a short amount of time.

Fish

2 Several of the worlds that Mario visits have water in them, which can be really difficult to navigate. Your best option is to use Cappy to possess a nearby fish, as it enables you to swim more easily and not worry about breathing. Just be careful when approaching dry land.

Chain Chomp

3 There are plenty of blocks in certain areas that Mario can't break open. Use Cappy to possess a Chain Chomp though, and you'll be able to smash them open with ease, hopefully finding a precious Power Moon in the process. You'll also need to possess one to defeat Madame Broode.

Moe-Eye

4 These weird, stone-like creatures can be quite hard to use because of how slowly they move. Stick with them, though, because when you use their sunglasses you will reveal pathways that are impossible to see. Memorize them and they will soon lead you to any nearby Power Moons.

Goomba

5 Using a Goomba is the only way to get the Power Moons held by the lady Goombas found on each world. They also have the ability to stack on top of one another, so they can be used to reach out-of-the-way locations that Cappy and Mario otherwise wouldn't have access to.

TIPS & TRICKS

Attack everything
You'll be amazed at what you can possess in *Super Mario Odyssey* so make sure you throw Cappy at everything.

Explore
Many of *Odyssey's* Power Moons are well hidden, so make sure you look in every nook and cranny if you want to find them.

Boss battles
A lot of the bosses you encounter have specific attack patterns, so make sure you master them in order to completely defeat them.

Master the controls
Some sections don't let you use Cappy's powers, so make sure you've fully mastered all of Mario's normal moves first.

Choose your enemy
Some enemies are more useful to possess than others. Always be aware of your surroundings so you choose the best one.

MEET THE SUPERFAN

MATT HENZEL

Who?

Matt Henzel is a huge video game fan and first started gaming in 1977 on the Atari 2600. He started collecting games beginning with the ColecoVision, but soon moved over to other systems. He's a huge fan of *Mario* games and has been collecting *Mario* games since the early 1980s. The very first game he purchased was a tabletop version of the *Donkey Kong* arcade game, which featured Mario, or Jumpman as he was then known. The first proper *Mario* game that Matt owned was the NES port of *Mario Bros*, another old arcade game that featured the popular plumber, along with his brother, Luigi. He's been collecting *Mario* games ever since.

Why?

Matt feels that *Mario* games are so much fun to play because they always make the best use of Nintendo's current hardware and they always look bright and colorful. He's also a big fan of the controls in *Mario* games, because they are tight and responsive. If he had to choose his favorite *Mario* game he'd have to side with *Super Mario World* on the Super Nintendo (also available on the SNES Classic Mini) as it has "everything you could ask for in a *Super Mario* game". His obsession with *Mario* continues to other memorabilia and he has extensive merchandise that ranges from T-shirts and books to posters, music CDs, and Amiibos.

ODYSSEY'S BEST WORLDS

Sand Kingdom

This world is an early desert stage and takes place in the city of Tostarena. You'll need to use Pyramid Coins to unlock the special suits that are found here.

Seaside Kingdom

The city of Bubblaine has a French theme, and is inhabited by a very angry, giant octopus. To unlock Mario's costumes here you'll need to collect Purple Shells.

ALSO CHECK OUT . . .

Rayman Legends: Definitive Edition

This is another enjoyable platformer, which is available exclusively on Switch. It's an enhanced remake that features bonus characters from earlier versions of the game, as well as touch-screen support.

DID YOU KNOW?

In previous games, coins were used to grant Mario an extra life if 100 were collected. They're now used to buy neat things from shops.

THE EXPERT SAYS . . .
DARRAN JONES
Editor, *Retro Gamer*

I've been playing *Mario* games for over 30 years. I've been wowed by early adventures and appalled by some terrible spin-offs, but one thing has always been consistent: the platform games are always brilliant fun. *Super Mario Odyssey* ranks alongside *Super Mario Galaxy*, *Super Mario World* and *Super Mario 64* as one of the greatest platform games ever made, and it's a testament to Nintendo's development teams that they keep coming up with fresh, exciting ideas for the iconic mascot. Cappy's ability to possess enemies puts a new spin on the game, enabling you to interact with each sprawling level in a way that wasn't possible in earlier *Mario* games.

Luncheon Kingdom

This fantastic-looking world reminds us of *Cloudy with a Chance of Meatballs 2*. You are able to unlock a chef's outfit by collecting Polygonal Tomatoes in the city of Mount Volbono.

Metro Kingdom

This world is clearly based around New York, and has distinctive *Donkey Kong* and construction themes. Mario can collect City Coins here to unlock costumes, and also meet *Donkey Kong's* Pauline.

Crash Bandicoot N. Sane Trilogy

This brilliant exclusive for the PlayStation 4 is great value for money, as it features enhanced versions of the first three *Crash Bandicoot* games. All three games will take an age to complete.

Super Lucky's Tale

The sequel to *Lucky's Tale*, this charming platformer stars a cute little fox called Lucky who is attempting to rescue his sister. It's available on both Xbox One and PC and really is fantastic fun to play.

DID YOU KNOW?

Chuchel was designed by artist Jaromír Plachý who previously worked on tricksy point-and-click adventure game *Botanicula*.

HAVE A CHERRY GOOD TIME

CHUCHEL

How much do you like cherries? Even if they are your favorite fruit, it turns out that there's someone who likes them even more than you do. Chuchel, the angry hairball star of this mobile and PC game, is positively obsessed with cherries, and, unfortunately, has had his cherry stolen from him. The good news is that it's up to you to try and claim it back, as you travel together through a brightly colored world of crazy characters and sounds. *Chuchel* is a puzzle game with a truly furious hero who only wants his cherry back, but this turns into a huge quest starring aliens, huge snails, yetis, and dangerous ladybugs. He might be a hairball of very few words, but he's not giving up until he gets his favorite fruit back in his stick-like arms. Just give him a hand, will you?

STATS

0 TIMES Chuchel actually speaks

53,000 VIEWS ON YOUTUBE FOR THE FIRST TRAILER

4 DIFFERENT DEVICES YOU CAN PLAY ON

1 STONE INSIDE CHUCHEL'S FAVORITE FRUIT

Cherry icon by Novita, speaking icon by Melo

TOP 5 CHUCHEL MOMENTS

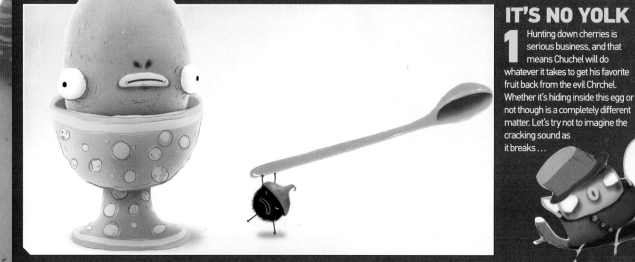

IT'S NO YOLK

1 Hunting down cherries is serious business, and that means Chuchel will do whatever it takes to get his favorite fruit back from the evil Chrchel. Whether it's hiding inside this egg or not though is a completely different matter. Let's try not to imagine the cracking sound as it breaks …

SEEING IS BELIEVING

2 Just because Chuchel can see his prize doesn't mean it'll be easy to get. You must tap on everyone and everything to see how the world interacts with your hairball. It won't just be a case of wandering over and grabbing that cherry.

MEET KEKEL

3 We all need friends to be there for us and simultaneously fight with us over cherries. Chuchel's small, pink buddy is called Kekel, and while he *should* be fighting in our hero's corner, he might want the cherry for himself, so you'll have to keep an eye on him.

READY YETI?

4 This sleepy (not to mention exceptionally grumpy) yeti is just one of the interesting characters you'll meet in *Chuchel*. There's also a pool monster hosting a party inside his own body, aliens from space, and a brilliant giant snail who has a built-in arcade. You'll have a *shell* of a time.

LAUGHTER IS THE BEST MEDICINE

5 Some levels have puzzles for you to solve, but there are also areas in which Chuchel is just beaten. The ball of fur will make you chuckle as he stomps on his hat in rage or gives up and climbs into a box.

ALSO CHECK OUT . . .

Botanicula
It might not have the same number of cherries or the angry hairball himself, but *Botanicula* is also from Amanita Design, and packed with comedy and puzzles as you quest to save a seed from evil parasites.

Machinarium
Amanita Design has also been rather busy with this beautiful point-and-click adventure game, in which you need to help a robot called Josef on his quest to save his girlfriend. Make sure you bring brain food, though—it gets hard.

TOP 10 FUNNY CHARACTERS

Crash
Crash Bandicoot: N. Sane Trilogy

2 There's a special place in a lot of hearts for Crash. Fortunately his hilarious nature is preserved in the excellent *N. Sane Trilogy*, meaning we get to experience his comedy stylings all over again. Honestly, look at that face and tell us you don't want to start laughing immediately.

Wheatley
Portal 2

3 *Portal 2* is still brilliant and a big reason why is the main enemy you face—Wheatley. Basically a fool, Wheatley becomes convinced he can become a great robo-leader when in actual fact he's . . . well, as we already said, a fool. But he really is. With his foolishness comes some of gaming's funniest lines, though. Bonus!

The Goat
Goat Simulator

1 Ah, the humble goat. No chance this could be a comedy character, right? Well if you say that you obviously haven't played *Goat Simulator*, one of the finest examples of a comic main character ever created. With its sticky tongue, love for rocket boost packs, and ability to destroy pretty much everything it encounters, the goat is relentless, unstoppable hilarity all the way from start to finish.

1 IT'S ALL IN THE EYEBROWS
If you spot a character who likes to wiggle their eyebrows, you're usually onto a funny one. It's the comic sidekick, boiled down to one feature. Check those eyebrows.

2 THEY'RE OVERCONFIDENT
Think Captain Qwark from the *Ratchet & Clank* series, whose overconfidence in very dangerous situations always ends with him looking incredibly foolish. Without his confidence, there'd be no comedy!

3 THEY TALK A LOT
Check out your comedy sidekicks in gaming and what's the one constant? They all talk a lot. That's because without throwing as many words out there as possible, how are they supposed to hit you with as many jokes as they can? Makes sense.

6 WAYS TO SPOT A FUNNY CHARACTER

4 THEY MAKE YOU LAUGH
This sounds very obvious, but what we actually mean is they make you laugh on purpose. There are plenty of characters who are funny by accident, but it's only those who do it intentionally you should look out for.

5 THEY'RE COWARDS
This has a few exceptions, of course, but generally speaking your comedy sidekick (this doesn't apply if they're the hero) is also a bit of a coward when it comes to taking on the enemy. Don't be ashamed to laugh along as they run away screaming.

6 THEY'RE NOT USUALLY THE BAD GUY
Sidekicks? Yes. Main characters? Of course. But the big bad guy? Rarely. There's no time to be the funniest person around when you have plans to conquer the world, so it's rare to see a funny character who's also your main enemy.

Cappy
Super Mario Odyssey

8 Cappy himself isn't the funniest part here—it's what he can do that makes us all laugh. From turning Mario into electricity to possessing a snoozing T-Rex, Cappy's powers might not have been intended to be funny, but they get us laughing anyway. He even lets us turn into a tree, which is superb.

The Director
Jazzpunk

9 When you have a boss giving you missions, you probably don't want someone as ridiculous as the Director in charge. Ridiculous missions that hardly make any sense eventually lead to the Director himself being turned into an alligator—and all the time you'll be howling with laughter.

The Rabbids
Mario + Rabbids: Kingdom Battle

4 The Rabbids have been created solely to be annoying and funny, but with *Kingdom Battle* they come into their own as hilarious, wacky characters. Being loud and yelling all the time is one thing, but doing it while dressed as Princess Peach is sure to have you doubled over with the giggles. Happily, the game is really good too!

Captain Qwark Ratchet & Clank series

10 He thinks he's the hero of the universe, ready to take on all comers and put the bad guys in space prison . . . except he's really not. Captain Qwark is and always has been a fool—sometimes out for himself, other times out for the good of the universe, but always a comedy genius, whatever it is he might be doing in any particular level.

Sans
Undertale

5 *Undertale* is a delightful game that's well worth playing, with plenty of memorable characters throughout. One stands out in the shape of Sans, the pun-loving skeleton. His jokes are intentionally bad, but when they're delivered with such passion it's hard not to laugh along with them.

Octodad
Octodad

6 One of our longtime favorites, *Octodad* is pure comedy from start to finish. He's an octopus in a suit pretending to be a regular guy with a wife and kids, and he almost does a good job . . . until he has to walk anywhere, pick anything up, open a door, or avoid a sushi chef —then the real craziness begins.

You!
Overcooked!

7 While we're very fond of *Overcooked!*'s raccoon chef, it's actually you, the players, that are the funniest part of this game. Watch as you start to get stressed and shout at each other, and drop those fries into the frozen ocean again, and fall off that truck, and make each other laugh endlessly!

THE EXPERT SAYS . . .
ROSS HAMILTON
Editor and video game writer

Sharp writing and great voice acting are often the keys to creating funny video game characters, and when done correctly they can turn a good game into a great one. *Portal 2* is a fun and ingeniously designed puzzle game, sure, but it's the witty dialogue and fantastic performances behind troublesome AIs GLaDOS and Wheatley that make it truly memorable. Sometimes characters can be funny purely thanks to their animation, too. The hero of *Octodad* might not say much, but it's impossible to keep a straight face when the game's purposefully tricky controls send you flailing across the screen, turning a trip to the grocery store into a hilarious slapstick routine.

OVERWATCH

THE WORLD COULD USE MORE HEROES

It's not very often we see a game instantly launch into a global success and manage to carry on that momentum into the future, but Blizzard managed it when it unleashed *Overwatch* onto consoles and PCs in 2016.

No longer just a game, today the *Overwatch* franchise has expanded to incorporate a comic series, short films, and an eSports league. It has become a franchise that can go toe-to-toe with the likes of *Star Wars*, *Pokémon*, and the Marvel Cinematic Universe.

Over *20 million* gamers have taken to the battlegrounds of Ilios, Hanamura, Dorado, and more—that's more than double the population of New York City. With updates, seasonal events, and more heroes being regularly added to the game, *Overwatch* continues to go from strength to strength and shows no signs of slowing down.

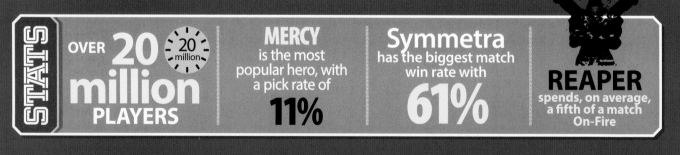

STATS

OVER **20 million PLAYERS**

MERCY is the most popular hero, with a pick rate of **11%**

Symmetra has the biggest match win rate with **61%**

REAPER spends, on average, a fifth of a match On-Fire

TOP 5 HEROES

Overwatch has a fantastic roster of heroes. Here are the best

1 Tracer

This time-bending hero features on the box art for good reason: she's awesome. Tracer's abilities encapsulate the Muhammad Ali quote "Float like a butterfly, sting like a bee" perfectly. Her short-range teleports and time warps keep her opponents guessing, while her twin-machine pistols and sticky bomb make her a force to be reckoned with.

2 Mercy

A team is useless without a good support keeping them healthy, strong, and—most importantly—alive, and Mercy is the best medic this side of Switzerland. Her healing staff can keep you topped up with health, and it can also give you the damage boost you need to break through your opponent's defenses.

DID YOU KNOW?

Take a look around the Eichenwalde castle and you'll find a bonfire that looks identical to the ones seen in the *Dark Souls* series.

3 Reinhardt

We could just say that Reinhardt uses a rocket-powered hammer and just drop the mic and walk off, but he's more than his iconic weapon. He's the definitive tank character, the shield to your sword, the protector of the squishies. You know you're safe when you hear this crazy German ironclad is by your side.

4 D.Va

You'd think that D.Va was all mech and nothing more, but no: she packs a punch when she's on-foot, too. Still, she's at her best when she's inside her giant robot, obviously. Her miniguns can keep constant fire on your enemy, while her ultimate self-destruct ability can completely obliterate an enemy team.

5 McCree

Cowboys are cool. Cigar-chomping aside, McCree's abilities make him really tough to go up against. He can dodge roll and instantly reload, and then throw a stun grenade in your face before he mows you down with his trusty revolver. All this while looking as cool as Clint Eastwood.

TIPS & TRICKS

Play the objective
Racking up Eliminations rarely wins matches. Get on the payload and capture the zones if you want to win.

Balance your team
Stop insta-locking Hanzo and take a look at what your team needs, not what you want to play.

Be positive
It's easy to get frustrated when you're losing, but remember it's a game: you're supposed to be having fun.

Take a break
If you're losing too many matches in a row, just walk away from the game for a bit. Coming back with a fresh perspective will help a ton.

Protect your support
They keep you alive, so the least you can do to pay them back is not let them get absolutely annihilated on the battlefield.

MONSTER HUNTER: WORLD

BRILLIANT BEASTS AND HOW TO SLAY THEM

With a name like *Monster Hunter* you'd think Capcom's insane beast-slaying series would be super popular. And it sort of is—mostly in Japan, though. The series made a name for itself by being ideal for commuters on the train; they could boot up their PSP or 3DS, hunt a wyvern for ten minutes or so, and be done in time for their stop.

Elsewhere, the series has a loyal, if smaller, fan base, and Capcom is hoping its latest release on home consoles will blow the series up and help it reign supreme like it has in the East for over a decade. *Monster Hunter: World* has more of a focus on co-op, with online play being easier on a home console, and a bunch of gameplay systems that are easier to understand than its predecessors.

STATS

5 games in the main series & **8** spin-offs

Over **40 MILLION** sales for the entire series

THE *MONSTER HUNTER* SERIES SPANS **14** YEARS and **9** CONSOLES

14 WEAPON STYLES IN *MONSTER HUNTER: WORLD*

TOP 5 HUNTING STYLES

It's all about the weapons

GREATSWORD

1 The Greatsword is the strongest weapon type in *Monster Hunter: World*; due to its size it's slower than a snail riding a tortoise, but it packs a meteor-strength punch and will deal plenty of damage. It's also a pretty safe choice for beginners.

SWORD AND SHIELD

2 This is the weapon style you want to go for when you start the game—S&S is as versatile as they come. You can basically mash buttons and it'll be fine, and you have a strong uppercut combo that you can use to mount monsters and cause problems.

HEAVY BOWGUN

3 There are three types of ranged weapons in *World*, but the Heavy Bowgun is by far the best. It can fire off the strongest ammo types, and each one has a special ability that can turn the weapon into a hose for bullets or a long-range sniper rifle, for example.

HAMMER

4 This thing is a great choice, especially for beginners—then again, it *is* a giant hammer. It is brilliant for breaking off armored parts from monsters. For example, if you're hunting something with an armored forehead, hit it with this powerhouse and it'll fall right off.

HUNTING HORN

5 The Hunting Horn is a weird one. It's best used for co-op play as you can use it to queue up songs and assist your allies. That said, you can still hit a monster with it like a mini version of the hammer. You'll surely make a lot of friends online if you master shredding this weapon, though.

ALSO CHECK OUT . . .

Toukiden 2

It's sort of like *Monster Hunter: World*, but with Oni demons instead. It borrows a lot from Capcom's iconic series, so you will be right at home here if you enjoy slaying monsters with outlandish weapons.

Dauntless

Developed by former *League of Legends* developers, *Dauntless* is a free-to-play action RPG for PC. Players must hunt Behemoths, collecting loot to level up their weapons to battle ever larger beasts. Well worth your time.

HELLO NEIGHBOR

WHAT IS THAT GUY UP TO?

The idea behind *Hello Neighbor is that you've moved into a new house and, across the street, a strange neighbor seems to be hiding a secret.* Your goal is to try and sneak into his house, and find out just what it is he is hiding. You've got to be careful not to be caught, of course. If you are, you'll be sent back to your house, and have to start all over again!

One of the coolest things about the game is that the neighbor will learn from your actions. He will set traps and take different approaches to counteract your tactics as the game goes on. That makes getting to the end of this sometimes-silly, sometimes-scary, stealth game, and uncovering the neighbor's secret, a little trickier than you might have thought.

STATS

17
Achievements to unlock on PC or Xbox

Consists of **3** EXCITING ACTS

The game . . . **HAD 4 ALPHAS** during development

Spent **2 YEARS** in early access

TOP 5 STEALTH GAMES

The best sneak-'em-ups out there

GUNPOINT

1 Whether hanging from the ceiling while an unsuspecting guard wanders past, or hacking a building's electronics to distract them, there are loads of sneaky tools at your fingertips in this awesome stealth game.

INVISIBLE, INC.

2 This strategy title is a thinking person's stealth game where you can take your time planning your next move, though that doesn't mean it's not very tricky! When everything goes according to your plan and you manage to lead your team of agents to success in a mission, it feels fantastic.

VOLUME

3 The guards in *Volume* always follow established patterns, allowing you to hatch a plan about how to get past them. That is, unless you decide you need to make a bit of noise to pull them off their path and give yourself an opportunity to slip by.

DID YOU KNOW?

Hello Neighbor had an unsuccessful Kickstarter that fell short of its $100,000 target. Thankfully, publisher tinyBuild picked up the game.

THE SWINDLE

4 The buildings you'll be breaking into in *The Swindle* are randomly generated, meaning the game is different every time you play. After every successful heist, you can use the spoils to upgrade your equipment and help you take on tougher challenges.

MONACO: WHAT'S YOURS IS MINE

5 Up to four players can play together in this sneaky heist game. There are eight characters to choose from, each of whom has its own special ability. The Locksmith can open doors twice as quickly as other characters, and the Mole can dig holes through walls, for example.

ALSO CHECK OUT . . .

Not The Robots

You play as a robot and must sneak around in an office, eating as much furniture as you can without getting caught. Achieving your objective without leaving yourself exposed is a difficult balancing act.

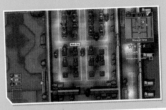

The Escapists 2

Although not strictly a stealth game, your job is to escape from a variety of cleverly designed prisons without getting caught. Play by yourself or with three friends to plan, craft, and, where necessary, fight your way out.

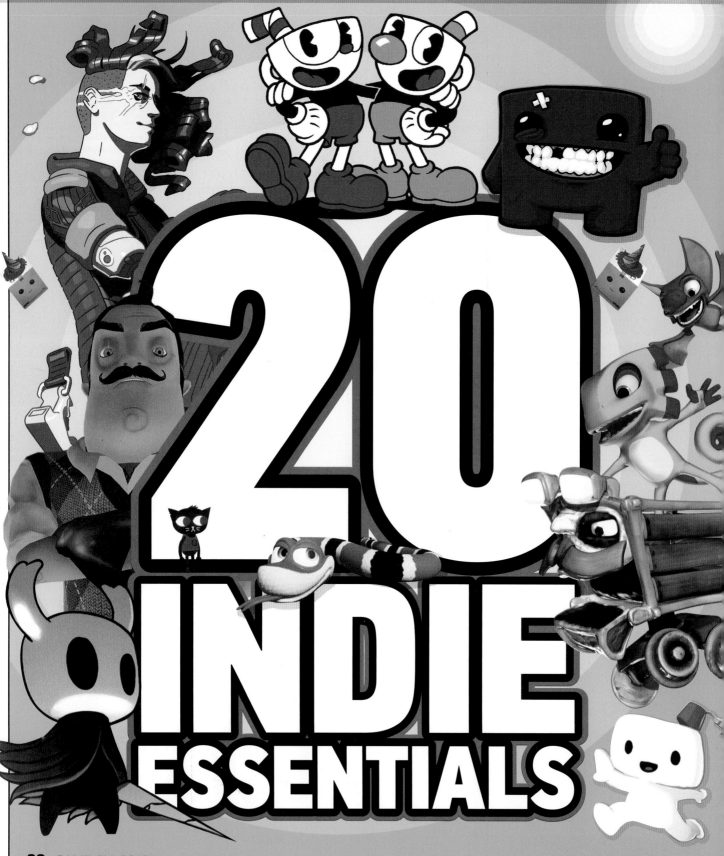

20 INDIE ESSENTIALS

Every week there seems to be another amazing indie game launching—it's definitely the place where the coolest, most interesting, and most inventive stuff appears. Without indie gaming, we'd have no *Minecraft*, no *Terraria*, and no *Spelunky*, so it's always worth investigating what gems are out there. Here are 20 of the absolute best—you'll definitely find something you'll love!

UNBOX: NEWBIE'S ADVENTURE

20 This cool 3-D platformer is just about the best thing you can do with a cardboard box. Your job is to bounce and roll your box, called Newbie, through the game's three awesome worlds. The corners of the box make for some tricky controls, as you're never more than a few seconds away from tumbling back down to earth.

HELLO NEIGHBOR

19 This is a bit of a creepy one. You have to break into your neighbor's house and figure out what he's hiding there—just don't let him catch you, or you'll be in for a world of trouble. This is one of those games that's as good to watch as it is to play. So tense!

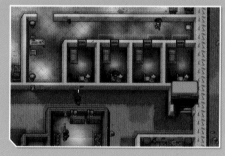

THE ESCAPISTS 2

18 The sequel to one of the smartest and most popular indie games of all time is packed with even more to do and even cleverer ways to get out of prison. Don't let the simple graphics fool you, though—this is a real challenge and a genuine head-scratcher.

GETTING OVER IT WITH BENNETT FODDY

17 This became big on YouTube because it's funny to watch your favorite players rage at how difficult it is. You're a man in a cooking pot, using a weird grappling hook thing to try and climb a very difficult set of obstacles. You can't die, but you can fall. All the way back to the beginning. Again and again and again.

BRAWLOUT

16
Why wait for *Smash Bros.* on Switch when you are able to get some battling action right now in *Brawlout*? If you're a *Smash* fan, you know what to expect, but this cool new selection of characters, and powerful, explosive moves make *Brawlout* almost as fun as the Nintendo favorite.

"COOL NEW CHARACTERS, AND POWERFUL, EXPLOSIVE MOVES"

GOLF STORY

14
Half golf game, half RPG, all charm. This hilarious mix of genres comes all the way from Australia and has you completing quests using your epic golfing skills, because in this world, almost every problem can be solved with a good putt. It's also very funny—a real hole in one!

A HAT IN TIME

15
It's been a big year for 3-D platformers, and even 3-D platformers about hats! *A Hat in Time* isn't quite as amazing as *Super Mario Odyssey*, but it's still funny, bright, bold, colorful, and a bunch of fun to play. It gets quite tough towards the end, though, so be warned!

NEX MACHINA

13
Developer Housemarque has been making some of the slickest shoot-'em-ups of all time since the 90s, and *Nex Machina* might be its best game yet. The aim is to blast wave upon wave of enemies into a million little pieces, while trying to rescue humans; the challenge is immense but so satisfying, and it never lets you take a break. The real excitement comes from going head-to-head with your buddies—can you be the best out of your friends?

HOB

12 The team that brought you *Torchlight* and its sequel returns with this very interesting action adventure, where you solve puzzles, battle enemies, and uncover mystery. *Hob* is a more thoughtful game than most, and has an amazing atmosphere. Underrated and well worth your time.

CELESTE

11 The creators of the amazing *Towerfall* created this incredible single-player platform adventure. Guide Celeste to the top of a giant mountain, through hundreds of inventive and tricky platforming challenges. Perfect controls, great graphics, and amazing music make *Celeste* one of the truly essential indie games of recent times.

SNAKE PASS

10 He may look cuter than Pikachu in a Santa hat, but this smiley snake is nothing but trouble. If you are skilled enough, you can twist this slippery guy around the levels using careful nudges of the analog stick. Move too fast, though, and he'll slink back down to the bottom of the level, and you'll have to "scale" those dizzy heights once again.

COOLEST INDIE CHARACTERS

Meat Boy Super Meat Boy

One of the original indie heroes, and star of perhaps the greatest 2-D platformer of modern times. Spawn, jump, die, repeat. He's a squishy, squelchy superhero.

Mugman
Cuphead

Cuphead's brother is basically the same person, but he has a better name. Who doesn't want to hang out with someone (some cup) called Mugman? Exactly.

Spelunky Guy
Spelunky

He's had the worst luck— boulders, spikes, bats, snakes, and man-eating plants—but comes back for more. What a hero. And he's back again in *Spelunky 2*.

Gomez
Fez

He may only be a few pixels high, but he's the star of one of the best indie games of all time. He's a puzzle-solving genius, a platforming wizard, and friendly too.

Shovel Knight
Shovel Knight

He's a knight. With a shovel. He uses that shovel to bounce on enemies' heads and explore his series of games with skill, power, and a lot of awesomeness.

NIGHT IN THE WOODS

9

If you like to experience a bit more of a story in your indie gaming, then this tale of animals in college might just be for you. There's not a lot of action in *Night in the Woods*, however, it's a very funny, smart, and entertaining experience that could be the ideal break from your usual gaming time.

YOOKA-LAYLEE

8

Another 3-D platformer, and one that feels like a retro classic. You play as a little green gecko called Yooka, who has a crazy bat friend called Laylee. You must track down countless pages from a magical book to take down an evil corporation.

RIME

7

If you ever played *Journey* or *Abzu*, you'll love *Rime*. It has a few more puzzles than the aforementioned games, but it tells a beautiful story, and features stunning visuals and sound. It's a little longer than *Journey* and *Abzu* as well, meaning *Rime* is an adventure you can really get stuck into.

PORTAL KNIGHTS

6

What do you get if you cross *Minecraft* with an action RPG? *Portal Knights*! Take all your crafting and building skills from years of playing *Minecraft*, and bring them here. You can craft buildings, fortifications, and even weapons, and then take on epic boss fights in this huge, never-ending sandbox.

SUPERFLIGHT

5

This amazing game has flown under the radar, but you can pick it up now super cheap on Steam. It's a wingsuit game where you fly as close to the scenery as possible, across an infinite number of randomly generated maps. What happens if you crash? Just try again.

HOLLOW KNIGHT

4

A stunning-looking 2-D platform exploration game, with one of the most unique art styles we've seen in a game. Everything is hand-drawn so looks super-cool, and the game is full of mystery, surprises, and all sorts of horrible insects to battle.

LAZARUS

3 A 2-D space blaster that's also an MMO? That's *Lazarus*, the ambitious project from Spilt Milk Studios that uses future-tech to build amazing worlds, which thousands of players can explore, while trying to defeat each other. It's certainly one of the coolest games out there for fans of multiplayer action.

THE EXPERT SAYS...
ANDREW SMITH
Founder, Spilt Milk Studios

Making an MMO is hard. Tens of thousands of players will play it every day for years, so we must write loads of story and characters, invent hordes of bad guys to fight, and design mysterious places to explore and cool treasures to find. For a team as small as ours, it'd be impossible.

With *Lazarus*, we designed the game around our limitations. The world resets and rebuilds itself every week, so it stays fresh— players must re-learn the location of favorite stores or enemies. Every time you die, you lose your equipped items, which forces you to choose what to head out into battle with. It's about making sure playing the game over and over is fun and interesting.

STARDEW VALLEY

2 What's cool about farming? EVERYTHING! *Stardew Valley* starts off like a simple resource-management game. However, it gets deeper and deeper, you start meeting crazy characters and making amazing friendships, and your farm gets enormous. A true indie classic.

CUPHEAD

1 Never has there been a more stylish game, and perhaps a harder game. *Cuphead* takes those classic cartoons from nearly 100 years ago and turns them into a super-hard platform/shooter, where you and (if you like) a co-op partner take on the craziest, coolest bosses ever created. You need a lot of patience to do well in *Cuphead*, so if you're the type of gamer who loses their cool too quickly, then maybe try something else. But if you think you can handle it, you won't find a better indie game this year.

DID YOU SEE THAT?!

SUPER MARIO ODYSSEY

In the first world of the game you will meet Cappy, a magic hat that can possess enemies and objects, and that Mario can also jump off! The combinations of jumps and cap maneuvers that Mario can perform with Cappy allow him to get to places both high up and far away, which he couldn't reach before. The in-game tutorial shows you how to do some basic moves, but here are some advanced techniques that are easier than you think.

1 As you wake up in the Cap Kingdom, Cappy will flee towards the bridge. Go here to talk to him and he will transform into your trusty red cap. The game will explain a few basic controls. We recommend using motion controls as it makes some moves easier to perform.

2 Flicking the right Joy-Con will throw the cap. If you are targeting an enemy and you miss, flick the Joy-Con towards yourself and Cappy will homing-attack the nearest enemy. Throwing both Joy-Cons in the same direction will make Mario throw the hat around him in a circle.

3 For a long jump, press ZL while running, quickly followed by A or B. For a higher jump, ground-pound by jumping and hitting ZL while in the air and then hit the jump button again as soon as Mario hits the ground. This will enable you to reach higher or further platforms than a regular jump.

4 For even longer jumps, throw Cappy while in mid-air and quickly tap ZL before holding the Y button. This will cause Mario to dive towards the hat while it is in the air and bounce off it. You can perform this twice in one jump but Mario won't bounce off Cappy the second time.

FIFA 18

BACK OF THE NET

Every year we wonder how *FIFA* can be improved, and every year EA Sports finds a way. *FIFA 18* is yet another world class entry to the series, with some key new gameplay features added to go along with the already overflowing collection of teams, players, stadiums, and modes. Team Styles mean that your favorite soccer team plays like they do in real life.

Assembling your Ultimate Team is still as engrossing, and features new Squad Battles, but make sure you take a break from Career Mode and FUT to enjoy the return of The Journey, too. The single-player mode once again puts you in the boots of Alex Hunter, and features some brilliant challenges as well as star-studded cameos from a selection of the world's greatest players.

STATS

OVER **700** playable teams

75+ stadia, including **50 fully licensed grounds**

94 Cristiano Ronaldo's in-game rating

1.6 MILLION players online simultaneously in **October 2017**

TOP 5 WONDERKIDS

Sign these young guns up and reap the rewards

1 KYLIAN MBAPPÉ

After his breakout season for Monaco and high-profile move to PSG, Mbappé has quickly become the hottest talent in world soccer. He's already a great forward in *FIFA 18*, with electric pace and superb dribbling skills, but it's his untapped potential that makes him a frighteningly good prospect.

2 MARCO ASENSIO

It takes a special type of player to keep the likes of Gareth Bale and Isco out of the team, but Marco Asensio is already managing it at Real Madrid. He's brilliant as a creative force when played in attacking midfield, but his impressive long shot rating means he's always a threat from distance, too.

3 GIANLUIGI DONNARUMMA

He might still be a teenager, but Gianluigi Donnarumma has already established himself as one of Europe's premier goalkeepers, and he's as effective in *FIFA* as he is for AC Milan. With a dual rating of 88 for both diving and reflexes, it'll take something special to score past him.

4 GABRIEL JESUS

Manchester City's Brazilian striker took no time at all to find his feet after a big-money move to the English Premier League, and he's one of the most well-rounded young forwards available in *FIFA 18*. His overall 81 rating might seem a little low, but his potential tops out at 92.

5 CHRISTIAN PULISIC

Pulisic is a huge threat to any team he's against thanks to his high dribbling skill, control with both feet, and movement stats. You'll be running rings around the defenders and setting up goals with ease.

TIPS & TRICKS

Size matters

Tall goalkeepers have a huge advantage in *FIFA 18*, so make use of the likes of Asmir Begovic and Jack Butland and their awesome reach.

Stay on your feet

Slide challenges may feel satisfying, but they leave gaps for the opposition to exploit—and a poorly timed one can leave you down to ten men.

Don't skip training

Training mode might not be the most exciting part of *FIFA 18*, but the drills can help you hone some of the game's most important skills. Just like real soccer!

Try the app

The free FUT smartphone app is a slick and convenient way to manage your team on the go. Check it out and you'll be able to keep constant tabs on your team from anywhere!

Home-grown heroes

Make the most of the Youth Academy in Career Mode—it can be a great source of cheap young talent down the line.

DID YOU KNOW?

The theme tune to *Madden NFL 18's* Longshot story mode is co-written by ex-NHL star Theoren Fleury.

MADDEN NFL 18

IT'S CLOBBERIN' TIME!

The big new feature in *Madden NFL 18* is a brand-new story mode called Longshot. Just like *FIFA's* The Journey mode, it sees you taking control of a fictional character on their quest to reach the big time. You find yourself competing in everything from high-school flashbacks to TV show challenges throughout 23-year-old Devin Wade's story, making important decisions to help shape the future of his career. Longshot is made possible by *Madden's* new Frostbite Engine, which also results in the best-looking NFL game to date. The gameplay is better than ever, too, adding new Game Styles and Target Passing to help provide more customization options this time around. Combine it all with the returning Ultimate Team, Franchise, Play Now Live, and other popular modes, and you've got yourself a really action-packed game of football.

STATS

32 NFL TEAMS

3 brand-new Game Styles

1st MADDEN to use Frostbite Engine

32 songs on soundtrack

TOP 5 TEAMS TO PLAY AS

Pick your favorite from these top football teams

NEW ENGLAND PATRIOTS

1 Looking for the best team in the game? Tom Brady's New England Patriots fit the bill, boasting an outstanding offense backed by the talents of superstar Tom Brady. Due to their incredible ability in *Madden NFL 18*, expect to face the Patriots regularly in online competition. Everyone will want a piece of this action.

HOUSTON TEXANS

2 For those seeking a superb defensive unit in *Madden NFL 18*, the Texans are a great choice. Much of that is down to superstar JJ Watt, who has outstanding attributes in strength and awareness in the game. Can you lead Houston to the Super Bowl in Franchise Mode?

DALLAS COWBOYS

3 Dallas fans will have to make do without Cowboys legend Tony Romo in *Madden NFL 18* following his 2017 retirement. The team still possesses outstanding talent, however, backed by the ability of Ezekiel Elliott, Zack Martin, and Dak Prescott. With these stars in your team, success is within reach.

ATLANTA FALCONS

4 Ahead of *Madden NFL 18*'s release, the Atlanta Falcons fell agonizingly short at Super Bowl LI, losing in overtime despite leading the New England Patriots 21-3 at the halfway mark. This is your chance to seek payback in Franchise Mode.

GREEN BAY PACKERS

5 If you prefer passing to running, the Packers are a great choice for use across all game modes. Star quarterback Aaron Rodgers has outstanding throwing power and accuracy skills in-game, while many of the Packers' offensive stars, such as Davante Adams, enjoy great catching stats.

TIPS & TRICKS

Choose your game style
Each of *Madden NFL 18*'s Game Styles (Arcade, Simulation, and Competitive) has a big affect on gameplay, so pick wisely.

Practice your playbook
All 32 teams come equipped with unique playbooks. Take time to practice your chosen playbook for a huge in-game advantage.

Take risks online
Don't be afraid to throw on fourth down and try surprising plays. Taking risks makes you less predictable.

Be humble in Longshot
You're required to make various decisions in Longshot. Being humble and kind improves Wade's rep.

Try Target Passing
If you're an advanced *Madden* player, check out Target Passing. This new game feature allows you to manually aim your throws.

GAME ON!

NBA 2K18

WELCOME TO THE NEIGHBORHOOD

DID YOU KNOW?

The game's cover had to be changed after release following Kyrie Irving's trade to the Boston Celtics.

NBA 2K18 **is possibly the most ambitious basketball game of all time.** Not only does it provide smoother animations, improved graphics, and more fun-filled gameplay than ever before, but it adds an entirely new open world to play around in. The Neighborhood takes the form of an in-game hub, allowing you to hang out with your friends and take part in cool activities. You can play pick-up games, visit retail stores, and even progress your MyCareer story, all with the goal of achieving a 99 overall rating for your created character. You can spend hours in the Neighborhood alone, while elsewhere, the ever-popular MyTeam, MyLeague, and MyGM game modes return with some big improvements. The world's best basketball game just got even better, and there's never been a better time to shoot some virtual hoops.

STATS

62 CLASSIC TEAMS ➡ **30** ALL-TIME TEAMS

900 unique MyTeam schedule challenges

13 IN-GAME BROADCASTERS

TOP 5 NEIGHBORHOOD AREAS TO VISIT

THE PLAYGROUND

1 This is the ultimate hangout, allowing you to play random pick-up games with other online players. You can participate in 2v2 or 3v3 matches, and it all counts toward your ranking, badge earnings, and virtual currency. Don't forget to bring your friends along for some help, too.

DOC'S BARBER SHOP

2 You can customize your character's appearance in all sorts of ways, and that includes a trip to Doc's Barber Shop. Here, you can trade virtual currency for a hairstyle of your choice, but pick wisely, as you'll need to earn more VC if you end up changing your mind.

2K ZONE

3 This is the perfect destination for relaxing away from the court, allowing you to participate in 2K Trivia, play mini basketball, and even try out your mixing skills at the DJ Booth. Don't forget to visit the JBL section, which offers a range of headphone accessories for your character.

PRO-AM TEAM ARENA

5 If you're ready to team-up with your friends online, check out the Pro-Am Team Arena. You can customize your team's branding, arena, and uniform before heading out to the court. Alternatively, visit the Pro-Am Walk-On Arena to match with random players.

G TRAINING FACILITY

4 Upgrading your player to a high rating isn't easy, but you can speed up the process by practicing outside of games. The best way to do this is via the Gatorade Training Facility, which offers a selection of gym-based activities such as squats, box jumps, and treadmill running.

ALSO CHECK OUT . . .

NBA Live 18
This is EA Sports' take on the world of basketball and it offers lots of appealing features, including an Ultimate Team mode, Franchise Mode, and The One—a single-player mode that is very similar to NBA 2K's MyCareer feature.

NBA Playgrounds
If you're looking for a less realistic take on the NBA, this arcade-style game is packed with huge dunks and high-scoring games. It's very similar to the 1993 classic and its 2010 remake, NBA Jam.

DID YOU KNOW?

Everybody's Golf used to be known as *Hot Shots Golf* in North America—the name might have changed, but it's still the same series.

EVERYBODY'S GOLF

IT'S GOLF—FOR EVERYBODY!

Golf is usually the best way to spoil a nice walk, but in the case of *Everybody's Golf*, it's one of the best ways to spend your time on the PS4. You don't have to be a golf enthusiast to enjoy the action, and there's—surprisingly—more to do than just hit balls down to the green (though that is great fun).

This being the 20th year of *Everybody's Golf* games, it should come as little surprise that Clap Hanz, the studio that has been making the games almost as long as they have existed, has produced a minor masterpiece. Taking your created character on a journey from golfing rookie to majors master is a fun journey, made all the better by the huge amount of online players to go head-to-head with. It's not the most realistic in the world, but *Everybody's Golf* is a brilliant representation of the sport.

STATS

8 courses in the game, which you unlock as you get better

12 games in the *Everybody's Golf* series (on all four PlayStations)

36,000 VIDEOS ON YOUTUBE ABOUT *EVERYBODY'S GOLF* ON PS4

THREE different ways of getting around—running, swimming, and *driving!*

TOP 5 CLUBS

The clubs you'll need to master to become a major player

1W (DRIVER)

1 Without this awesome club you wouldn't be making any progress on any of the courses. You usually use the driver to tee off at the start of a hole, but sometimes it can come in handy when you're on the fairway—it's not an all-rounder, but you can't get by without it.

PUTTER

2 When you finally make your way to the green, you'll want to get a more accurate club out. Step forward the putter. This flat-faced club allows you to hit limited distance, accurate shots across short grass. Don't try and use it anywhere other than the green, though!

SW (SAND WEDGE)

3 We'll always end up in the sand traps at some point. Which is where this savior steps in—the sand wedge is made to cut the ball out from the sand and put it back in a more favorable position. This is the club that we're most grateful for.

5I (IRON)

4 Here's your all-rounder—the club that works in far more situations than you might expect. The five iron doesn't hit the ball super-far, nor will it get your ball out of the worst situations, but it is usually helpful and almost always appropriate for any given situation.

PW (PITCHING WEDGE)

5 When you're used to your pitching wedge, you can use it to grab more chip-in birdies—that is, hitting the ball in the hole from outside of the green—therefore making your golfing look even more spectacular. The glory club!

ALSO CHECK OUT . . .

The Golf Club 2
If you're not particularly enthusiastic about over-the-top golfing action, don't worry—*The Golf Club 2* is a straight-faced simulation of the sport. You won't be doing super backspin shots, but it's still a lot of fun.

Mario Golf: World Tour
Another light-hearted take on golf, this portable version for the 3DS is actually made by the studio that made the very first *Everybody's Golf* game back in 1997. Oh, and it's fun too!

TOP 10 POWER UPS

The Shield Potion
Fortnite: Battle Royale

1 Finding the right loot in *Fortnite* is imperative to your survival. Throw in the fact you've got 99 other players to contend with and you can imagine how difficult not insta-dying is. When you first land, you'll want to keep an eye out for a blue potion bottle. This handy item applies a small shield, meaning you can withstand a few extra hits before being dropped.

Super Sonic
Sonic Mania

3 The *Sonic* series can be pretty unforgiving at times (take the Egg Robot in *Sonic 2*, for example). Thankfully, there is a way to turn the tables. By entering through hidden rings in *Sonic Mania*, and capturing all the UFOs, players unlock Super Sonic; an all-powerful, invincible speed demon who can blast through levels and enemies quicker than you can say 'Chili Dog'.

Smash Ball
Super Smash Bros.

2 *Smash Bros.* is a frantic, fast-paced brawler. But the moment a smash ball appears, you can bet every player will be climbing over each other to grab it. This item bestows a final smash attack. Use said attack and you'll send your opponents flying off the screen, turning the tide of battle in your favor.

6 TIPS TO IMPROVE ONLINE

1 NO I IN TEAM
Always be sure to work alongside your team. Although you may want to act like The Rock and go off by yourself, there's always strength in numbers. A well-coordinated team succeeds more than it fails.

2 COMMUNICATE
Whether you're on voice chat or communicating via in-game text, communication really is vital. Always call your tactics and plans before you execute them so that your team can be there to follow through.

3 KNOW WHERE YOUR TEAM IS
Always be aware of where your team is and team up to outnumber enemies. Keep track of where the healers in your team are. They need protecting and you may need to run back and grab a heal.

4 IT'S OKAY TO LOSE
It's important to try and understand why you lost without blaming others. Did you miss many shots? Was your team too spread out? Use losing as a means of improving your performance.

5 AVOID BEING MEAN
We all get angry online, but what's the point? Shouting or sending mean messages doesn't make you play better, it makes you less focused. Be gracious in defeat!

6 KEEP YOUR COOL
It's been proven the more relaxed you are, the better the team performs. Saying someone did something great motivates them. Screaming down the mic when someone fails doesn't.

Sentinel
Destiny 2

4 What's the one thing missing from *Destiny 2*? That's right, Captain America. In *Destiny 2*, after progressing through the story, players can unlock the Titan class Sentinel. Build up the special bar, and your Guardian pulls out a hard-light shield to boomerang into distant enemies for some damage.

Orbs
Altered Beast

5 Back in the olden days, when dinosaurs roamed the Earth, Sega released *Altered Beast*. While it wasn't to everyone's tastes, it did feature a cool idea: collect enough orbs and the character transforms into a monster. Namely a werewolf, a bear, or a dragon that shoots electricity!

Boxing Glove
Super Bomberman R

6 The boxing glove power up lets the player hit a bomb over in-game tiles. So if you're in a one-on-one and there are tiles between you and the other player, drop a bomb, punch it, and watch as it travels over the tiles and straight to the other player.

Power Pellet
Pac-Man

7 *Pac-Man's* not that great when it comes to powers. He's essentially a wheel of cheese with a piece missing who is afraid of ghosts. But when Pac-Man collects a power pellet, he ain't afraid of no ghosts. The ghosts turn blue and start running away, meaning they can be eaten by Cheese-Wheel-Man.

Cappy
Super Mario Odyssey

8 Technically not a power up, Cappy stands to be Mario's strongest companion to date. Have you ever seen an enemy and thought how cool it would be to play as them? Now you can. Simply line up a baddie, throw Cappy in their direction, and bam! You now have control of them.

Heart Containers
The Legend of Zelda: Breath of the Wild

9 Okay, spoiler: there aren't any heart containers in *Breath of the Wild* as such. Or at least, they aren't found in the wild. Instead, you'll need to beat four shrines to gain orbs, then visit a Goddess statue to trade in those orbs for either a heart container or a stamina boost. The more hearts you have, the more health. Meaning less getting one-shot by overpowered enemies.

The Blue Shell
Mario Kart 8 Deluxe

10 The dreaded blue shell is either the best or the worst power up depending on your perspective. This item, when thrown, will zoom through the racetrack in search of the person in first, before soaring into the air and crashing down in a fiery explosion. All the race leader can do is sit and watch as everyone overtakes them. Warning: The blue shell can end friendships and should be used with caution.

KINGDOM HEARTS III

EVERY STORY MUST COME TO AN END

DID YOU KNOW?

The biggest and best bosses in *Kingdom Hearts III* are based on famous Disney enemies, and are as impressive to behold as they are to battle.

One of the craziest collaborations in the history of gaming, *Kingdom Hearts* sees the worlds of *Final Fantasy* and **Disney collide.** *Kingdom Hearts III* is actually the 12th installment in the action-RPG series, bringing closure to a story almost two decades in the making. Returning hero Sora joins up with a host of popular Disney characters. Together they journey through some iconic worlds in search of the seven Guardians of Light as they attempt to thwart Master Xehanort's plan to start a second Keyblade war. If that all sounds like nonsense, that's okay, because *Kingdom Hearts III* is guaranteed to be a good time even if you aren't caught up with the story. Wild action, a deep story, and a hearty mixture of loveable characters ensure that this will be one unmissable and endearing adventure that should be enjoyed by all.

STATS

5 YEARS how long the game has been in development

7 GUARDIANS OF LIGHT

12TH GAME IN THE SERIES

FINAL CHAPTER *of the* **DARK SEEKER SAGA**

TOP 5 CHARACTERS

The key players in *Kingdom Hearts'* twisting story

SORA

1 The hero of *Kingdom Hearts III*, Sora has overcome so many trials over the last two decades, though this will be his final adventure. With his trusty Keyblade in hand, Sora will join up with a band of heroes and friends to do battle against the Heartless.

DONALD

2 Donald Duck is a powerful magician in the incredible world of *Kingdom Hearts* and a direct assistant to King Mickey. Donald will make his return to help bring harmony to the land alongside Sora as the Heartless make their final push for dominance.

GOOFY

3 Who'd have ever thought that Goofy would be anything more than a loveable, well, goof? Well, in *Kingdom Hearts* he is a famed captain of the Royal Knights and a powerful ally to Sora, bringing the group together to help return King Mickey to safety.

RIKU

5 While he was once a foe, Riku has quickly become an unlikely friend to Sora. After shaking the darkness of Maleficent, Riku is now busy helping the group defeat the Heartless and assisting in the search for Sora's bestie Kairi—missing ever since the Destiny Islands were invaded.

HEARTLESS

4 One of the main antagonists of the *Kingdom Hearts* series, the Heartless are manifestations of the darkness that is found in people's hearts. If left unchecked, the monsters threaten to engulf all of the world in darkness and send it into chaos.

ALSO CHECK OUT . . .

LEGO Dimensions
If you're a big fan of the crossover element of *Kingdom Hearts III* you really should check out LEGO *Dimensions*. It draws from a huge amount of properties for a pretty amazing adventure.

Disney Magical World 2
Looking for even more of your favorite Disney characters to come together in gorgeous, familiar worlds? *Disney Magical World 2* is a fun game that should satisfy any desire to spend more time with these characters.

DID YOU KNOW?

Sonic didn't start off as a hedgehog, but rather a brave rabbit that could use its ears to throw objects at enemies.

BLINK AND YOU'LL MISS HIM!

SONIC THE HEDGEHOG

Who is covered in blue fur, has serious attitude, and wears some pretty sweet red running shoes? Sonic the Hedgehog, of course, Sega's long-standing mascot. After almost three decades of totally rocking the video game world, he's not showing any signs of slowing down. And why should he? He's still the fastest video game character on the planet!

Throughout the years, Sonic has starred in a bunch of great games, and now he's back in *Sonic Mania* on PS4, Xbox One, and Nintendo Switch. Harking back to the classic 2-D side-scrolling games of old, this is a real return to form for Sega's super-speedy mascot after some recent disappointments. Players can take control of Sonic or one of his trusty companions—Tails or Knuckles—as they aim to defeat their evil nemesis Dr. Eggman and his Hard-Boiled Heavies.

STATS

The first *Sonic* game began development in **1990**

There are **30** STAGES in *Sonic Forces*

2 Number of tails that Tails has

OVER **350 MILLION** $$$ *Sonic* games sold

TOP 5 SONIC GAMES
The best of the trusty Sega mascot's games

SONIC ADVENTURE 2

1 Dash into one of Sonic's earliest 3-D romps! This fast and fun entry has you racing along mossy jungle treeways, raising adorable Chao pets, and even outrunning a rampaging semi-truck. Plus you can play as Shadow, Tails, Knuckles, and also Rouge the Bat, one of the lesser-known *Sonic* characters.

SONIC FORCES

2 Ever wanted to make your own custom *Sonic* avatar? *Sonic Forces* lets you do just that, as well as take your creation on an exciting adventure alongside a small army of *Sonic* pals. Sprint your way through both 2-D and 3-D levels while jamming to one seriously rocking soundtrack.

SONIC MANIA

3 A recent release that's a true tribute to the classic 16-bit Genesis titles, *Sonic Mania* is mostly 2-D and relies on intense side-scrolling action for all of its stages. Great for gamers who want to experience Sonic's retro roots but in a modern, polished way.

SONIC & ALL-STARS RACING TRANSFORMED

4 Sonic is pretty extreme on his own, but seat him in a shape-shifting vehicle and things start to get really crazy. Drift around in a car, ride the ocean waves in a boat, then sprout wings and launch into the clouds.

SONIC COLORS

5 You'll have to dig out your old Wii or Wii U to play this hidden gem. Guide Sonic through a glowing space theme park on his mission to free small alien creatures called Wisps from the clutches of Dr Eggman.

ALSO CHECK OUT . . .

Yooka-Laylee
This retro-inspired 3-D platformer has you taking control of best friends Yooka (a green chameleon) and Laylee (a purple bat) on a quest to retrieve the stolen pages of their magical book.

Crash Bandicoot N. Sane Trilogy
Three classic *Crash Bandicoot* titles come together in one brilliant modern package, all remastered from the ground up with shiny new graphics. These games are tons of fun, but beware—they can get extremely challenging!

LEGO MARVEL SUPER HEROES 2

MINIATURE HEROES, BIG ACTION!

It's time to save the universe by traveling through time and space! All of your favorite Marvel heroes get a brick-tastic makeover in this action-packed game. When evil villain Kang the Conqueror brings cities from different time periods and even different realities together, he creates Chronopolis and declares himself the ruler. Thankfully, the superheroes came with them, and now you have to bring them together to help defeat the evil Kang and send the cities back to where they belong!

You can run, punch, and fly your way through some of the most famous locations from the Marvel universe, including Black Panther's Wakanda, New York, and even the Old West. You can explore all of these places in the huge open world of Chronopolis as any hero you like—and there are hundreds to unlock!

STATS

18 different locations in Chronopolis

4-player in competitive multiplayer

| 1 | 2 |
| 3 | 4 |

OVER **200** characters to unlock

255 gold bricks to unlock

TOP 5 SUPER HEROES

Take control of your favorites

ROCKET & BABY GROOT

1 Everyone's favorite alien duo are back in this game, and Groot has a cool trick. Because Kang the Conqueror has been messing with time, Groot can grow and shrink really fast, allowing him to slip through small gaps, or smash everything up as a fully grown Groot!

SPIDER-MAN NOIR

2 This alternate-reality version of New York's web slinger comes from Marvel's Noir universe, set in 1933. He has all the same powers as the normal Spider-Man, but with his retro costume and awesome flying goggles, this hero is super-cool.

GHOST RIDER

3 Johnny Blaze, aka Ghost Rider, made a pact with the evil Mephisto in order to save his father's life, but he was tricked. Now he uses his special powers to defeat evil. He can reach high places with his Grapple Lift ability and also shoot beams of heat.

DID YOU KNOW?

The hyphen in Spider-Man's name was put there by his creator, Stan Lee, to make it look different from Superman.

HULK 2099

4 Not to be mistaken with Bruce Banner's Hulk, and how could you with those lizard-like features? As well as having the power to smash through enemies, he can also launch himself right into the air, making for some fast getting around.

SQUIRREL GIRL

5 This charming (and surprisingly powerful) hero can use her big, bushy tail to attack enemies, and has sharp claws that you can use to dig up buried items in the game. She's also super strong, and can throw explosives that will blow up the silver bricks that you find.

ALSO CHECK OUT . . .

LEGO Star Wars: The Force Awakens

Relive the heroics of *Episode VII* in LEGO form with this brilliant adaptation. The epic adventure lets you play as famous heroes from the movies, and fly awesome ships like the Millennium Falcon.

Yooka-Laylee

There may not be any superheroes in this platforming title, but it's packed with well-designed levels, funny characters, and items to collect. Heroes Yooka and Laylee have some cool powers, too!

STREET FIGHTER V

NEVER GIVING UP

One of the great things about *Street Fighter V* is the way Capcom has been keeping the game fresh. There's been a stream of cool new characters to download, giving us new moves to learn, abilities to play with, and favorites to help us rise up the rankings.

Capcom has taken that a step further with the release of the Arcade Edition—free to download for anyone who has the base game. This edition adds a new Arcade Mode, an Extra Battle Mode, and a second V-Trigger ability for each character.

With these regular updates and new characters, an already fantastic fighting game has become even better, and continues to hold our attention by giving us new ways to play. It feels like *Street Fighter V* is never going to get old.

STATS

Record for most Evolution Championship entrants with

5,000 registrations in 2016

THE 8

FINALISTS at EVO 2017 used **8 different characters**

28 characters included with Arcade Edition

NO. 1 for prize money in the Evolution Championship Series

TOP 5 DOWNLOADABLE CHARACTERS

The coolest characters added to the core *SFV* roster

1

BALROG

It was great to see this favorite, who made his debut all the way back in *Street Fighter II*, make a return as a DLC character. Balrog is considered a top-tier character in *Street Fighter V*, so he should serve you well when it comes to getting wins online.

MENAT

There have been plenty of old favorites returning as downloadable fighters, but it's cool to see something new too, and Menat offers just that. Making her debut in *SFV*, Menat is an Egyptian-themed character who uses a floating crystal ball to attack her opponents.

2

3

URIEN

This powerful fighter, who made his debut in *Street Fighter III*, can be devastating in the right hands. Urien is able to create mirrors that can reflect projectiles back at your opponent, or be used to bounce them off to create cool combos.

IBUKI

This young ninja has speed and agility on her side, making her a tough character to pin down. She's also got a few ninja tricks up her sleeve, such as the bombs she can throw out to help her control space.

4

ZEKU

Zeku first appeared in *Street Fighter Alpha 2*, but he wasn't a playable character, so his *Street Fighter V* version is the first we've been able to play with. His V-Trigger ability transforms him into a younger version of himself with a different moveset.

5

ALSO CHECK OUT . . .

Arms

Just because Nintendo's colorful and cartoony 3-D fighter is a pleasure to look at, doesn't mean it doesn't have the depth to pack a punch. Expect some thrilling battles, whether you're playing with friends or online.

Dragon Ball Fighter Z

If you love fighting games and the *Dragon Ball Z* cartoon, it doesn't get much better than this. The game does a great job of capturing the epic, over-the-top battles the cartoon is known for.

GAMER CHALLENGE!

Why stop playing a great game when you've got to the end of the story or beaten the final boss? Instead, you can make your favorite games last even longer by beating these tricky challenges we've set for you. They will help to test your gaming skills to the limit, push you to try new things that will make you a better player, and reveal new dimensions to your favorite games that offer you whole new ways to play.

SUPER MARIO ODYSSEY (Nintendo Switch)

Clear a kingdom

Don't think *Super Mario Odyssey* is all over once you've seen the credits roll. That's just the start! Pick a kingdom and try to collect every single moon and purple coin it has. You'll soon realize that Nintendo has filled the game with cool ideas, tough challenges, and even secret kingdoms.

LEVEL UP!
Collect every moon

Once you 100% a kingdom, you're on the path to *Super Mario* mastery. Take your new high-level platforming skills and nose for finding hidden moons to other kingdoms to see if you can get all 999 available.

SCORE ATTACK

Just Dance 2018
(PS4, Xbox One, Nintendo Switch)

See if you can break 13k points on Ed Sheeran's *Shape of You* for a huge megastar rating.

DESTINY 2 (PS4, Xbox One, PC)

Tag-team a Nightfall

For the ultimate test of your *Destiny* skills, try to complete a Nightfall with only two players. They're built to be finished by a team of three, so it's going to be tough, but it can be done. Once you've done that, you could always try a solo run to prove your complete mastery of the game. Just remember, it'll probably take a couple of tries to complete this challenge!

FORZA MOTORSPORT 7 (Xbox One, PC) Unassisted

Forza 7 offers a whole range of assists to help make driving easier. Try turning them off one by one until you get used to driving completely unaided. Once they're all off, see if you can win the Forza Driver's Cup without any assists at all.

FEATURE

TIME ATTACK

Super Mario Odyssey
(Nintendo Switch)

Once you've beaten Bowser, go back and see if you can complete the game in less than five hours. It's tough!

STARDEW VALLEY

(PS4, Xbox One, Nintendo Switch, PC)
Old school

Look after your land in this fantastic farming sim the old-school way. That means you're not allowed to use sprinklers or fertilizers to manage your farm. Farming in this traditional way, see if you can complete the Community Center before year four. Nobody said organic farming was easy . . .

LEVEL UP!
Farm master

Prove that you've mastered *Stardew Valley* to the man that left you the farm at the start of the game. Get a full score of 21 points when Grandpa comes to evaluate you in year three and demonstrate that you're a true master farmer.

ROCKET LEAGUE

(PS4, Xbox One, Nintendo Switch, PC)
Rocket-powered MVP

To become a true *Rocket League* MVP, you need to master the art of scoring aerial goals. Start by getting used to using your boost to get into the air and hit the ball while it's up high. Once you get the hang of that, your next objective should be to start getting shots on target. Eventually, you'll score a spectacular aerial goal. Finally, see if you can net a hat-trick of high-flying aerial shots in one match. Even if you get halfway to completing this, you'll already be a better *Rocket League* player.

OVERWATCH

(PS4, Xbox One, PC)
All-rounder

Top the scoreboard with every single character on the *Overwatch* roster. The knowledge of *Overwatch's* characters and their different playstyles that you'll be forced to gain to complete this challenge is guaranteed to make you a better player. You might even find a new favorite to play as.

POKÉMON ULTRA SUN & POKÉMON ULTRA MOON

(Nintendo 3DS, Nintendo 2DS)
Trainer's challenge

There are two important rules to follow to complete this popular *Pokémon* challenge. First, if a Pokémon faints, you can't use it again. Second, you can only catch the first Pokémon you encounter in each area—if it escapes, you've missed your chance.

EXPERT CHALLENGE!

Crash Bandicoot N. Sane Trilogy
(PS4)

Clear one of the games from the trilogy without taking a single hit of damage. Go on.

FIFA 18 (PS4, Xbox One, Nintendo Switch, PC)
From rags to riches

Pick a team from the bottom of the pile—a team like Yeovil Town or Forest Green Rovers from England's League 2, for example—in career mode. Your challenge is to take this small team of strugglers up the soccer ladder and see if you can get them into the top division. If you're not familiar with many of the British teams in the lists, give them a quick Google and look for the ones that come from small towns and that rank low in the leagues. It'll be a real challenge to take them to the top . . .

LEVEL UP!

Best in Europe

Once you've taken your team to the top division, why stop there? See if you can win your domestic league and the European Cup to become the best team in the world.

DID YOU KNOW?

One of the minds behind *Final Fantasy XV's* story, Kazushige Nojima, was also a lead writer on *Final Fantasy VII*—arguably the best game in the series.

FINAL FANTASY XV (PS4, Xbox One, PC)
Defeat Adamantoise

Adamantoise is a powerful optional boss that will give you a tough challenge to work towards outside of completing the main game. It can be tackled from Chapter 9 onwards, after completing the sidequest Let Sleeping Mountains Lie. At level 99 and with 5,000,000 HP, don't expect it to go down easily.

LEVEL UP!
Beat all superbosses

Adamantoise isn't the only optional boss in *Final Fantasy XV*. Once you've defeated it, hunt down Ayakashi, Bilrost, Naglfar, MA-X Angelus-0, and the Dread Behemoth to complete the set.

EVERYBODY'S GOLF (PS4)
Birdie bounty

You're going to have to know a course like the back of your hand to get this one. Try to complete a whole course without getting anything less than a birdie on each hole. If that's too easy for you, get at least one Eagle and one Albatross too.

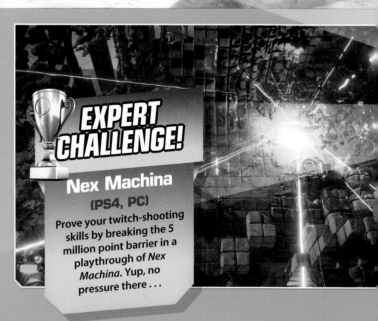

EXPERT CHALLENGE!
Nex Machina (PS4, PC)

Prove your twitch-shooting skills by breaking the 5 million point barrier in a playthrough of *Nex Machina*. Yup, no pressure there . . .

TOP 5 COOLEST CHALLENGES

SEA OF THIEVES
(Xbox One, PC)

Perfect teamwork

Prove that you and your friends are the greatest pirate crew to sail the seven seas. Your challenge is to complete three voyages in a row without anyone in your party taking damage. All of you will have to be at the top of your game, and watching each other's backs to do it.

CUPHEAD (Xbox One, PC)

Untouchable

Cuphead's tough enough as it is, but it's about to get even tougher with this challenge. Your task is to try to beat every boss in the game without taking a single hit. It might seem impossible, but it really can be done.

Rising up the ranks
Street Fighter V (PS4, PC)

Win five online ranked matches in a row. Nothing will make you feel cooler than defeating real players and moving up a rank.

No shield needed
The Legend of Zelda: Breath of the Wild (Nintendo Switch)

Complete the game without ever using a shield, proving that you've mastered its combat.

Go super
Sonic Mania (PS4, Xbox One, Nintendo Switch, PC)

Find all of the Chaos Emeralds to transform into the invincible Super Sonic. Collect all Emeralds, get 50 rings, jump into the air, then press jump again.

Try three against one
Star Wars Battlefront II (PS4, Xbox One, PC)

As the last one standing against a team that still has three players left, wipe out the opposing team.

Clear it out
Fortnite (PS4, Xbox One, PC)

Clear out a whole squad from a base they are defending without any help from your allies in *Fortnite's* squad Battle Royale mode.

MINECRAFT (PS4, Xbox One, Nintendo Switch, PC, Mobile)
Thrill ride

Put your mining and building skills to the test to create an awesome rollercoaster. The challenge isn't only in collecting all the precious redstone and other materials you'll need, but in putting all the moving parts together to create a thrilling ride for you and your friends.

LEVEL UP!
Under the sea

There's no truer test of your building skills than constructing an amazing structure in a difficult environment. Make a splash by building a cool Atlantis-style city that is entirely underwater.

EXPERT CHALLENGE!

The Legend of Zelda: Breath of the Wild (Nintendo Switch)

Complete *Breath of the Wild's* tough Master Trials DLC in three hours or less.

SPLATOON 2 (Nintendo Switch)
Coverage

You'll usually find that painted territory ends up closely split when playing *Splatoon's* multiplayer mode Turf War, but we're challenging you to change that. Team up to wipe the floor with your opponents by winning a match with 70 per cent coverage.

THE SIMS 4 (PS4, Xbox One, PC)
The legacy challenge

The *Sims* community loves coming up with ways to make the game more tricky, like the legacy challenge. Start with one Sim on an empty lot with only $2,000 of cash in the bank. Build up your home and start a family that goes on for ten generations.

RAIN WORLD

(PS4, PC)
Lore lover

Complete the side quest to fix Moon's memories and you'll open up new possibilities. Scour the world for colored pearls and bring them to Moon. Each one will unlock new bits of lore that will give you more detail on the world. See if you can unlock every bit of lore.

LEVEL UP!
Perfect run

If you've restored Moon's memory and unlocked every bit of lore, then chances are you're pretty good at *Rain World*. Let's see just how good: Can you finish the game without dying? And yeah, we do mean not even once.

SCORE ATTACK!

Thumper
Score over 200,000 points on the first level of this thrilling rhythm game.

1

2

NIDHOGG 2 (PS4, PC)
Whitewash

In *Nidhogg 2*, you start off face-to-face with your opponent, ready to do battle. Every time you beat them, you can push into the next screen along. When they beat you, they'll push back in your direction. The one who can push their opponents back through all their screens to the end of the stage wins the match (and gets eaten by a giant worm). Normally, there's a lot of back and forth in these battles, but there won't be if you want to complete this challenge. Your goal is to whitewash your opponent by pushing them all the way to the end of the stage without being pushed back a single time yourself.

3

TOP 5 CRAZIEST CHALLENGES

Beat 'em blindfolded
Dragon Ball FighterZ (PS4, Xbox One, PC)

Challenge a friend to a fight and beat them without looking at the screen. It can be done.

Eggplant run
Spelunky (PS4, PC)

Grab yourself an Eggplant and carry it safely all the way through the game to the final boss. You will be treated to a cool surprise. No, we are absolutely not going to tell you what it is.

Facing fears
Minecraft (PS4, Xbox One, Nintendo Switch, PC, Mobile)

Pretend your character has a fear. They could be scared of the dark and have to open up caves to explore, or scared of water and have to build a bridge to cross. Make them face it.

Controller crossover
Overwatch (PC, PS4, Xbox One)

Use controllers like they were never intended. Can you top the scoreboard with a DJ Hero turntable or a Rock Band guitar?

Pacifist run
Super Mario Bros (Wii U)

Fight against your Mario instincts and don't jump on anything! Your goal is to finish the game without harming a single enemy (apart from the final boss, Bowser, obviously).

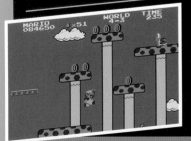

WORMS W.M.D
(PS4, Xbox One, Nintendo Switch, PC)
One trick pony

This challenge flips the way you play *Worms* on its head. Instead of having a huge list of weapons to choose from, you can only use the Bazooka for a whole match. See if you can defeat a friend or another player online using only that weapon.

OKAMI HD (PS4, Xbox One, PC)
Weakling run

Make your playthrough of *Okami HD* a whole lot trickier with this no-upgrade challenge. Aside from upgrades you get automatically through the story, avoid all health and ink upgrades and use only the first weapon from each class—and don't power them up, either. This challenge will add some extra excitement by making battles more difficult.

THE EXPERT SAYS...
AZORAE
Speedrunner

I've always been a pretty competitive person, and speedrunning allows me an interesting and unique outlet for that. It also allows me to meet other like-minded people and make amazing friends by both cooperating on speedrun planning efforts and competing in races and tournaments.

Games Done Quick events (twice-a-year speedrunning events raising money for charity) are another excellent part of being in the speedrunning community. Being able to meet friends from around the world while raising money for such a great cause is incredibly fun and rewarding.

TIME ATTACK!

Rayman Legends
(PS4, Xbox One, PC, Nintendo Switch)

Complete the invaded version of the Enchanted Forest in 35 seconds or less. We won't lie, the speed and reaction times you'll need for this take some practice.

THE LEGEND OF ZELDA: BREATH OF THE WILD (Nintendo Switch)
Solo survivor

For this challenge, you'll need to finish the game without getting any help from friends and allies. This means no buying or selling of any items. You can only survive on what you are able to scavenge in the wilds.

LEVEL UP!
Wilderness master

To take your survivalist run to the next level, drop all your clothes, weapons, food, and materials whenever you swap Tower zones. Survive only on what you can find in that area. This will really test your skills, but have faith, you can do it!

DID YOU SEE THAT?!

SONIC MANIA

The second level of *Sonic Mania's* Chemical Plant Zone appears to be your standard stage—you'll be speeding through when all of a sudden you're literally dropped into an entirely new **mini-game.** Those who've played past *Sonic* games might recognize this as Mean Bean Machine, or Puyo Puyo. If you collect 20 silver medals from the bonus stages throughout the game, you can unlock a two-player version of the mini-game. The goal is to fill your opponent's side with puyos until they can't place anymore.

1 At first everything seems normal. You pass a checkpoint like you would before any boss fight. Enter the tube, much like the others scattered around the level when you're dropped into a cube next to Dr. Eggman, where he has been waiting.

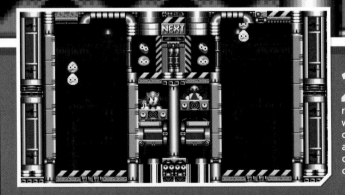

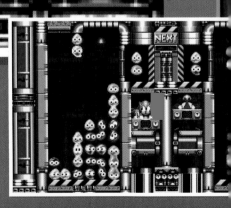

2 Puyos will fall from the top and you need to connect four of the same color to remove them. The only color that will not disappear when four are connected are the black ones. If a black puyo is touching another colored puyo that is being cleared, it will also be removed.

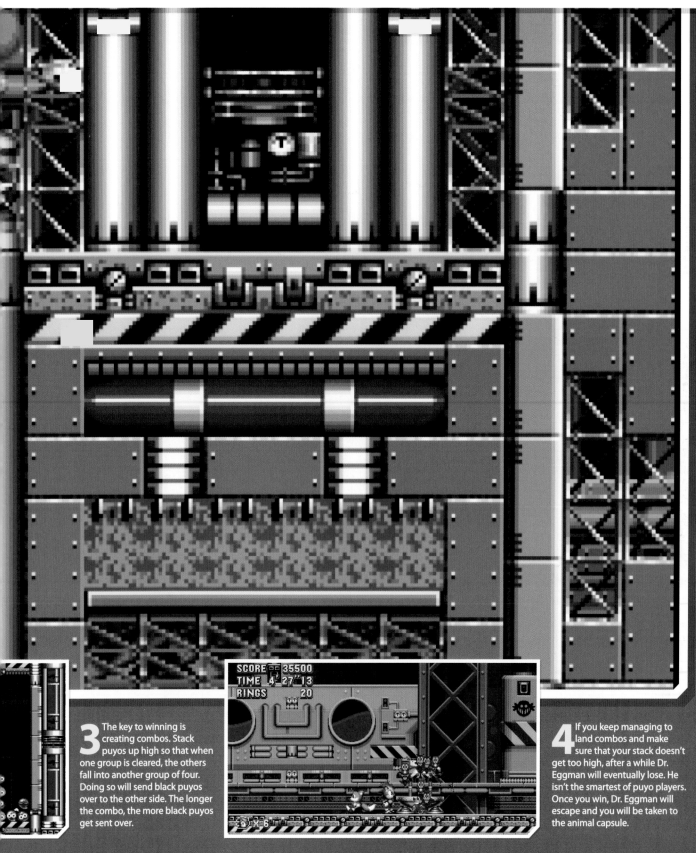

3 The key to winning is creating combos. Stack puyos up high so that when one group is cleared, the others fall into another group of four. Doing so will send black puyos over to the other side. The longer the combo, the more black puyos get sent over.

SCORE 35500
TIME 4'27"13
RINGS 20

4 If you keep managing to land combos and make sure that your stack doesn't get too high, after a while Dr. Eggman will eventually lose. He isn't the smartest of puyo players. Once you win, Dr. Eggman will escape and you will be taken to the animal capsule.

DID YOU KNOW?

You can ride bears and even mystical creatures in *Breath of the Wild*, but sadly you can't take them back to a stable and keep them as pets.

THE LEGEND OF ZELDA: BREATH OF THE WILD

A NEW HERO IS BORN

Take a step into the wild in Link's latest adventure. *Breath of the Wild* lets you explore the enormous kingdom of Hyrule as you work to stop the evil Ganon from taking over the kingdom. A hundred years ago, Link—helped by Princess Zelda and four guardians—locked Ganon away in Hyrule Castle. However, Link was badly injured and has been sleeping for 100 years in order to recover. When he wakes, he finds the kingdom he protected has all but forgotten him, and Ganon is breaking free! It's up to you to beat all of your enemies, collect powerful weapons, and finish the battle between you and Ganon once and for all. This epic game is now even better thanks to DLC that expands the story and adds fantastic new outfits and weapons to discover and use—plus there are plenty of awesome new challenges for you to face.

STATS

The first *Zelda* game was released **32** years ago

4.7 MILLION copies of *BotW* sold

124 SHRINES TO COMPLETE

15 armor sets to unlock in the base game

TOP 5 PLACES TO SEE
Take a Hyrule tour

Climb down

THE TEMPLE OF TIME

1 This ancient temple has appeared in several of the *Zelda* games. In *Breath of the Wild* it was attacked by Ganon, and is damaged when Link awakens. It's near to the start of the game, though, and holds some useful items, so it's worth visiting.

GORON CITY

2 The Gorons are rock-people that live on Death Mountain, and their city is full of interesting people to meet and things to see! You'll need to wear armor that protects you from the heat if you want to visit, though, so make sure that you're tooled up before you go.

Climb down

KOKIRI FOREST

4 This ancient forest has been a huge part of previous *Zelda* games, and it's the same in *Breath of the Wild*. You'll find the Great Deku Tree, who has been watching over the powerful Master Sword. When you're strong enough, you can pull the sword from the stone!

HYRULE CASTLE

3 The castle is a scary place to go, as it's packed with dangerous monsters and deadly goo, but it's worth the risk. The castle has a ton of powerful weapons hidden away inside, so if you're brave enough, you can get powerful swords and the strongest shields!

TARREY TOWN

5 After meeting Bolson in Hateno Village, he will disappear north to start a new town. When you find him later, you'll need to assist him by bringing other inhabitants to the town. It's worth helping out, because Tarrey Town is a beautiful place with some useful items to purchase.

TIPS & TRICKS

Use the weapons
When you find a powerful new weapon, don't be afraid to use it! You'll often find new ones, so you might as well make use of them.

Experiment with food
Try cooking up different recipes for different results. You can find new recipes on posters on the walls of stables.

Search for seeds
There are 900 Korok seeds to find, and they will help you expand your inventory. Grab them whenever you can!

Always have food
Prepare plenty of food to boost stamina and health—you don't want to get stuck with nothing to eat!

Utilize fire
Fire is extremely useful in *BotW*. You can use it to make updrafts for flying on, damage enemies, or burn away brambles.

Happy	Jazzy	Crazy	Funky	Sunny	Baby
GOOD	OK	SUPER	GOOD	GOOD	OK

JUST DANCE 2018
GET YOUR GROOVE ON

You can't beat a good boogie. *Just Dance 2018* returns with a brand-new set of tunes and moves for you to copy, with artists such as Ed Sheeran, Katy Perry, and Bruno Mars featuring on the tracklist. The brand-new Kids Mode comes packed with unique dances, while you can also take on the Dance Lab or compete online with the World Dance Floor. The best bit is that you don't even need a Kinect, Wii Remote, Joy-Con, or PS Move to play, as the Just Dance Controller app for Android and iOS devices can turn up to six players' smartphones into separate controllers (on current-gen consoles). With 40 new tracks to dance to and over 300 classics available through the Just Dance Unlimited package, the Just Dance catalog keeps getting bigger all the time.

STATS

40 new tracks

300 extra songs through Just Dance Unlimited

12 alternate routines to unlock

9 games in main *Just Dance* series

TOP 5 SONGS TO DANCE TO

Get your groove on to these hits!

AUTOMATON - JAMIROQUAI

3 The lead single from Jay Kay's 2017 album is all about technology, so you'll need to tap into your inner robot for this one! It's a dance packed with rigid, robot-like movements, and makes use of your entire body, from your head to your feet.

24K MAGIC - BRUNO MARS

1 The Hawaii-born singer-songwriter brings us a funk-filled treat with this one, making it impossible to keep your feet still! The dance, which is fairly easy to learn, takes the form of a duet, and can actually be practiced ahead of time via the free *Just Dance 2018* demo.

HOW FAR I'LL GO - DISNEY'S MOANA

4 This 2016 smash hit is a great fit for *Just Dance 2018*, and is the sixth Disney song to be included in the main series. It's a solo routine, packed with fun, exotic hula-style dance moves, making it perfect for the whole family to enjoy.

DID YOU KNOW?

The Nintendo Switch edition of *Just Dance 2018* features an exclusive "Just Mario" track and two-handed dance routines.

BEEP BEEP I'M A SHEEP - LILDEUCEDEUCE FT. BLACK GRYPH0N & TOMSKA

2 This ultra-catchy YouTube sensation has scored tens of millions of views, and it's easy to see why. The four-step routine has you throwing your hands in the air, bouncing around on the floor, and going crazy as you "beep beep like a sheep." Give it a try in Kids Mode.

ANOTHER ONE BITES THE DUST - QUEEN

5 Queen's classic foot-stomper is a four-person routine, but can be played with as many participants as you like. It's filled with energetic, workout-style moves, and if you want your dance to receive a "Superstar" or "Megastar" rating, you'll need to combine teamwork with outstanding individual skill.

ALSO CHECK OUT . . .

Dance Central Spotlight

This excellent Xbox One exclusive dancing game features tracks by artists such as Pharrell Williams and Rihanna. Unlike *Just Dance*, the game requires an Xbox One Kinect camera and features a huge library of DLC.

97,280

Disney Fantasia: Music Evolved

Also requiring a Kinect, *Disney Fantasia: Music Evolved* allows players to create and manipulate music with their body. Like *Dance Central*, it's developed by Harmonix—the same team behind the *Rock Band* series.

DID YOU KNOW?

Iden Versio, the star of the game's campaign, is played by Janina Gavankar, who has had multiple roles in movies and TV shows.

RETURN OF THE JEDI

STAR WARS BATTLEFRONT II

This superb space adventure gives you exactly what you want from a sequel: It keeps everything that was great about the first game and adds new layers that make it even better. Just as with the original, *Battlefront II* is a *Star Wars* fan's dream come true. It nails the sights and sounds of the series, making you feel like you've stepped into a *Star Wars* movie. This

time around the game has heroes, villains, and maps from every movie era. There are some great improvements to gameplay, too. Most importantly, *Battlefront II* introduces a class system that adds a tactical element to the game. This not only makes teamwork more important, it gives the game a layer of depth that keeps it interesting and makes you want to keep coming back for more.

STATS

14 playable heroes and villains at release

UP TO 40 SIMULTANEOUS PLAYERS IN GALACTIC ASSAULT MODE

5 MULTIPLAYER MODES AT RELEASE

BATTLEFRONT II'S CAMPAIGN CAN BE COMPLETED IN AROUND **5 HOURS**

TOP 5 NEW HEROES AND VILLAINS

Rey

1 It's awesome to have the new hero of the *Star Wars* series available to play in *Battlefront II*. Rey is a close-range fighter who's at her best getting stuck in with her lightsaber. She has a cool Jedi Mind Trick power that confuses nearby enemies.

Kylo Ren

2 Given that Rey is in the game, her nemesis has to be in there for her to go up against, too. Kylo Ren's Frenzy ability is great for taking down multiple targets—it allows you to leap from enemy to enemy, attacking with your glowing red lightsaber.

Darth Maul

3 One of the most powerful of the hero and villain characters in the game is Darth Maul. His trademark dual-blade lightsaber is great for close-range battles, but he's also got a trick up his sleeve for ranged attacks—his lightsaber hurling attack, Furious Throw.

Yoda

4 He may be loveable and funny at times, but this tiny Jedi Master isn't someone you should mess with. He can be a great team player, thanks to an ability that pushes back enemies, and another useful one that heals Yoda and surrounding teammates.

Lando Calrissian

5 Even putting his special abilities to one side, Lando can dish out a lot of damage with his blaster. With an ability to disrupt enemy radars and one that unleashes a cloud of smoke that he can still see through, he is also great at confusing your foes.

TIPS & TRICKS

Learn the classes
Try out every class to see which one works for you and to learn what their weaknesses are when you face them.

Don't overheat
Keep an eye on your blaster to make sure it doesn't overheat. Vent your blaster when you get a chance.

Play the objective
The objectives are the most important thing in multiplayer. You'll have much more success focusing on those than your own personal glory.

Spend your battle points
You'll gradually earn battle points during multiplayer modes. You can spend them to spawn a powerful hero or vehicle.

MEET THE SUPERFAN

Paul Hackett

JAMES BURNS

Who?

James is a writer and a huge *Star Wars* fan, who, in 2007, created his own fan site called Jedi News, which has become one of the biggest fan sites in the world. He also contributes to a number of other fan sites and co-hosts two podcasts.

How?

Star Wars has played a key role in James's life since he first saw the original movie in the winter of 1977. He has been an avid *Star Wars* collector and gamer ever since. He remembers getting *X-Wing vs TIE Fighter* and all the numerous add-ons for his PC in the 90s. Skip forward 25 years and he is very much enjoying the single-player campaign in *Star Wars Battlefront II*, along with all the additional free content and downloads made available to celebrate *Star Wars: The Last Jedi*.

MULTIPLAYER CLASSES

Officer

The Officer class is a support class. It has abilities that make allies stronger, and a handy deployable turret that is great for holding down mission objectives.

Assault

The Assault class are your frontline soldiers. They are great at close and medium range and are vital to help your team push through enemy defenses.

ALSO CHECK OUT ...

Fortnite

If your favorite thing about *Battlefront II* is its multiplayer mode and you're looking for more online action, then try the Battle Royale mode in this exciting shooter. It's fast and action-packed.

DID YOU KNOW?

Events in *Star Wars Battlefront II's* single-player campaign take place in the 30 years leading up to *The Force Awakens*.

THE EXPERT SAYS . . .
JOHN STANLEY
Designer at Criterion, developer of *Battlefront II's* Starfighter Assault mode

It all starts off [with] game feel. It's about how we expect a vehicle to handle. How do we expect an X-Wing to feel? Especially now with our class-based system, we think something like the X-Wing is our all-rounder, so we want it to be agile but not too powerful. Something like a Y-Wing, we want to be a bit more tanky and a bit slower, but it's going to be backed up by massive amounts of damage. It was looking at each different starfighter and how we thought it would feel and then . . . making it handle that way.

Heavy

This class makes up for what it loses in speed with power. Their ability to lay down a barrage of suppressing fire is a great help when defending.

Specialist

With the specialist, you don't want to go toe-to-toe with your enemy. This class's speciality is long-range sniping and traps to catch out foes.

LEGO Star Wars: The Complete Saga

Want more *Star Wars* but fancy something a bit more light-hearted? The LEGO series' hilarious version of the events of the *Star Wars* movies is sure to get you laughing every time.

Plants Vs. Zombies: Garden Warfare 2

It may not look like *Star Wars Battlefront II*, but under the cartoony graphics, you'll discover another fantastic class-based multiplayer shooter that rewards skill and teamwork.

CREATE YOUR OWN LITTLE NOOK

ANIMAL CROSSING: POCKET CAMP

Pocket Camp **is a fun, mini-look at the incredible world of** Animal Crossing**.**
With many of the main-game features transferring to your smartphone, you can now craft furniture, befriend villagers, fish, and catch bugs, all on the go at any time! This game will have you hooked from the beginning as you explore exotic locations, from Saltwater Shores to Breezy Hollow, trying to appease your new animal visitors by gathering their favored items and building the furniture in their chosen style. It's very straightforward and charming, attracting new and previous fans of the series alike. Some features have been stripped-down to help take *Animal Crossing* to the comfort of your smartphone, so that you can move around with your camper van and hang out with villagers like never before.

STATS

5,000 BELLS
The price of Tuna, the rarest fish in the game

44+ Villagers to befriend

15 million APP DOWNLOADS IN FIRST WEEK

790,000 bells needed in total to fully upgrade your camper

Fish icon by Martyn Jasinski

TOP 5 VILLAGERS

Our favorite cool villagers to befriend

KID CAT

1 This tom cat is a sporty, cool villager and a bit of a jock superhero, but his sense of justice rules above all. His name is a reference to DC Comics' Kid Flash, so it's no surprise that he will fight tirelessly to protect his town from evil.

RADDLE

2 Black and yellow Raddle resembles a poison dart frog. Despite being a lazy villager, he's friendly and easy to get along with. He wears a mysterious surgical mask all year round, but nobody knows why. Only one way to find out . . . become his friend and maybe he'll talk!

PHOEBE

3 A brilliant, beautiful, tall ostrich with a flame-patterned body and peacock-style vibrant feathers, Phoebe is a phoenix-inspired animal with a caring, big sister vibe. She knows the secrets to a long life, unsurprisingly, but recommends taking things slow and taking your vitamins regardless.

APOLLO

4 Bald-eagle Apollo shares his name with Apollo 11, the first manned spacecraft to land on the Moon. Coincidentally, his birthday is July, 4, or Independence Day! He can be a bit cranky, like the Greek god Apollo, but befriend him and he'll reward you with a guitar at level 10.

KETCHUP

5 With a bright red head and body, Ketchup resembles a round tomato, complete with the green leaf-shaped pattern on top of her head! Ketchup is very peppy and tends to get a bit overexcited or dramatic in conversation, most often when food, especially pizza, is involved!

TIPS & TRICKS

Perfect fishing
Save time by watching for the right-sized shadows; pale chubs, for example, tend to be the smallest shadow in Lost Lure Creek.

Trigger new catches
Couldn't find the bug or fish you want? Just speak to an animal in that area and the game will trigger new appearances!

Sell extra fruit
If you find you have extra oranges, try selling them in the Market Box to your friends.

Finding animals
If you want to make friends with an animal more quickly, just call them up on your Contacts list to get them to your camp.

Sweet talking
Don't worry if you've run out of quests for a visiting villager, you can still speak to them to gain experience and maybe even level up your friendship!

TOP 10 CRAZIEST GAMES

Getting Over It with Bennett Foddy

1 What's crazier than making a game to punish people? Nothing, probably. *Getting Over It* was made to punish everyone who plays it, making it the craziest game in memory. Players have to get themselves over a mountain, playing as a man in a large pot who climbs using a sledgehammer. It is absolutely infuriating, way too hard for its own good, completely crazy— and yet utterly compelling.

Kirby: Star Allies

2 When you're playing *Kirby: Star Allies* alone, the crazy factor doesn't come into play quite as much—but throw in three friends and you've got yourself a recipe for true madness! The four of you can band together to make your abilities even stronger—abilities like Friend Train and Friend Star might not sound too wacky on paper, but in motion it's a sight to behold.

Hatoful Boyfriend

3 Dating simulators might not be the most popular genre in modern gaming, but this is one everyone still talks about—it's the dating simulator where you go out with . . . birds. Genuinely funny, sometimes surprisingly heartfelt, and always crazy, *Hatoful Boyfriend* surprised everyone with just how well received it was. And now you can find it on mobile or Steam.

6 TIPS TO REMEMBER WITH CRAZY GAMES
Mad, bad, and useful to know

YOU'RE TRYING SOMETHING DIFFERENT
Always be open to new experiences, even with games—step outside of your comfort zone. There's no better way to do this than with crazy games!

YOU MIGHT NOT HAVE HEARD OF THEM
Generally speaking it's the "normal" games that get a lot of attention from your friends, YouTubers, and online! So you're actually digging a bit deeper.

SOME MIGHT BE TOO CRAZY
Just because it's crazy, doesn't mean you'll like it. It might not be something you enjoy—it might actually be too crazy for you. And that's fine, because at least you've tried it out!

THEY CAN BE VERY IMAGINATIVE
Because crazy games aren't what you might usually expect, developers can be a bit more experimental with the features. This can be good or bad, but it's fun!

DON'T JUST STICK WITH CRAZY
When you get into your crazy games, it can take over a bit —searching out that next zany experience and all. But don't be afraid to return to your usual games.

QUALITY DOESN'T MATTER
If you're playing something because it's crazy, it doesn't matter necessarily if it's not that good. Play it for the experience, so you have stories to share with your friends.

Goat Simulator

4 Running as fast as you can through a city, destroying everything in your path: it could only be *Goat Simulator*, one of the best crazy games ever made. Initially created as a joke, the game has since gone on to spawn many updates and expansions, each just as crazy as the last—and all just as much fun as you would expect.

PaRappa the Rapper

5 Ever wanted to learn karate from a man with an onion for a head? Do you want your driving instructor to be a moose? And would you turn to an angry chicken for baking tips? *PaRappa the Rapper* brings you all this craziness and much more besides.

Desert Bus

6 Created by Vegas magicians Penn and Teller, *Desert Bus* was originally one part of a package of games called *Smoke and Mirrors*. But it was the eight-hour drive across a featureless desert that got all the attention—and rightly so. It's intentionally a garbage game, meant to poke fun at the player—and it's available in VR on Steam.

1-2 Switch

7 One of the first games for the Nintendo Switch is also one of the craziest, with *1-2 Switch's* plentiful party games all ticking the silliness box. While air guitaring and quick drawing are fun, nothing beats milking cows for that pure craziness factor. Sure, it might draw some funny looks thanks to the motion-controlled nature of the game, but you'll be having too much fun to really care!

Headlander

8 Imagine a world where your head can be freed to fly around and do other things while your body carries on as normal. Sound crazy? Well it's exactly what happens in *Headlander*, in a futuristic sci-fi world where people have uploaded their consciousness into the cloud. Use your flying head to connect with and use different robot bodies to achieve different tasks.

DID YOU KNOW?

Headlander was developed by Double Fine Productions, the team behind the brilliant *Psychonauts*.

Space Giraffe

9 With over 30 years of crazy gaming behind it, Llamasoft released the action arcade game *Space Giraffe* on Xbox 360 and it was . . . brilliant. It was also crazy, in the best way. There's always something going on, you're always having your attention drawn from one place to another, the graphics are gorgeous, and the music is amazing.

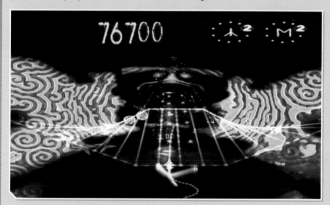

Octodad

10 You play this classic of crazy as an octopus in a suit who is pretending to be a human man—oh, also you have a wife and two children, and they don't know you're an octopus. It is, quite frankly, incredible. Learning to control Octodad as he makes his way around on dry land—not very graciously—is as frustrating as it is funny, but there's never any doubt in your mind about just how great *Octodad* is.

YO-KAI WATCH 2: PSYCHIC SPECTERS

MAKING FRIENDS WITH MONSTERS

Just as in the previous versions of *Yo-Kai Watch 2*—*Bony Spirits* and *Fleshy Souls*—in *Psychic Specters* you play as a young kid in the town of Springdale. As you explore the town, you befriend spirits called Yo-Kai and build a team to battle the evil Yo-Kai causing trouble in the town. However, *Psychic Specters* has a lot of cool stuff to do that wasn't in *Bony Spirits* or *Fleshy*

Souls. For a start, there's a new location to visit: a mysterious train that only shows up at night will take you to a theme park called Gera Gera Resort. It has rides, hot springs, and a theater. There are also new Yo-Kai to collect, new time-traveling quests that give you a look at the history of characters like Whisper, and new bosses to battle in four-player co-op mode.

STATS

There are **3** versions of *Yo-Kai Watch 2*

Almost **700** Yo-Kai in the main series

6 ranks of Yo-Kai from **E** to **S**

2 main characters to choose from. One **female** and one **male**

TOP 5 YO-KAI TO COLLECT

The must-have Yo-Kai to find in *Psychic Specters*

DID YOU KNOW?

If you have *Yo-Kai Watch 2: Bony Spirits* or *Yo-Kai Watch 2: Fleshy Souls*, you can transfer your save into *Psychic Specters* so you don't have to restart the game again.

JIBANYAN

1 Okay, Jibanyan might not be new to *Psychic Specters*, but as the first Yo-Kai you get to add to your team in every version of *Yo-Kai Watch*, we can't help but have a soft spot for him. He's the Pikachu of the *Yo-Kai* series.

ILLUMINOCT

2 New to *Psychic Specters* is Illuminoct. This is a powerful Yo-Kai that can take a lot of punishment, making it a great addition to your team. It is a lightning-based Yo-Kai that can use aggressive abilities like Voltage and Dragon Flash.

UNKEEN

4 Unkeen is one of the wicked Yo-Kai that play an important role as the bad guys in *Yo-Kai Watch 2's* story. After finishing *Psychic Specters*, he can be found and befriended in the Springdale Business Tower.

DARKYUBI

3 Another Yo-Kai that's new to *Psychic Specters* is Darkyubi. It is a Yo-Kai with the Drain attribute; it can drain health from enemies to heal itself. You can meet and befriend Darkyubi next to Sawayama Castle.

UNFAIRY

5 Unkeen isn't the only powerful Wicked Yo-Kai you can turn and recruit to your team. Again, you must finish the game to recruit this one, found close to the river in Prayer's Peak Tunnel after you've finished the game.

ALSO CHECK OUT . . .

Pokémon Ultra Sun & Pokémon Ultra Moon

Collecting, battling, catching 'em all . . . the latest additions to the *Pokémon* series are as excellent as you'd expect.

Ni No Kuni II: Revenant Kingdom

Yo-Kai Watch's battle system is pretty simple, so if you're ready to take your monster battling to the next level, then the second game in the popular anime-inspired *Ni No Kuni* series might just be for you.

DID YOU KNOW?

Fortnite's successful Battle Royale mode wasn't originally planned. It was added in 2017 and has taken the game to new heights.

FORTNITE

BUILD AND DESTROY

Fortnite **has evolved to become two great games.** It started off as a co-op survival adventure. In this mode, you explore, scavenge, craft weapons, build bases, and defeat monsters. However, the game now also has an awesome Battle Royale mode. Each match has up to 100 players—either solo, in pairs, or in four-player squads. Everyone starts with only a pick axe when they parachute onto the map. Once you land, it's time to start scavenging for weapons and resources, and building defenses with the goal of being the last one standing. You must stay in the safe area of the map, which gradually shrinks as a growing storm surrounds you, pushing players together. It's one of the most exciting multiplayer experiences out there right now.

STATS

Fortnite hit **40 MILLION** downloads in January 2018

100 PLAYERS IN A GAME OF BATTLE ROYALE

The game has achieved a high point of over **2 MILLION** concurrent players

First revealed **7 YEARS** ago, in 2011

TOP 5 LANDING LOCATIONS

Breaking down the game's best starting spots

TOWER

In the most northeast corner of the map is a tower that houses a number of chests. Land on top of the tower, work your way down, and when you've searched everything, head to the nearby ice cream truck to find more items for your haul.

RUSTY HOUSES

This one can be risky as there are multiple hiding spots that opponents could use. You're almost guaranteed to get one or two good weapons and some shield so you'll be ready to head towards the nearby Junk Junction to fight.

MOTEL

To the west of Anarchy Acres is a long motel, but this spot often attracts other players. Staying on the roof of the motel is always a good strategy as you can peak through holes in the ceiling and surprise anyone trying to hide.

LARGE TREE

There are nearly always two chests at the trunk of the tree and there's a weapon drop south of the tree on the high grounds. Once you've gathered equipment you can head south to overlook Tomato Town where you'll have a great view of wandering enemies.

MOUNTAIN

North of Salty Springs, located in the center of the map, is a multi-layered mountain with plenty of chests. It also offers multiple locations to visit once you've collected the equipment. Get to the chest at the peak of the mountain as quickly as possible to avoid getting picked off by snipers.

ALSO CHECK OUT . . .

Minecraft

The PC version has a host of servers dedicated to Battle Royale modes, and while *Minecraft*'s combat controls aren't as good as *Fortnite*'s, it can be manic fun.

Overwatch

While it's missing the battle royale element of *Fortnite*, *Overwatch* offers fantastic multiplayer fun. Team up with your buddies and work together to beat the opposition.

TOP 10 WAYS TO SECURE A VICTORY ROYALE

Gather all the resources you can

3 Everybody starts with one essential item—the melee pickaxe. It isn't particularly effective in a fight, but it *is* super awesome at helping you gather resources. Use it to smash and bash pretty much everything you come across to earn vital materials—wood, brick, and metal—as these will be key in the late-game as you begin building defenses to give you an advantage over your opponents.

Pick your landing zone

1 *Fortnite: Battle Royale* sees 100 players dropping out of the Party Bus and fighting for survival on a sprawling island—there can be only one winner. Your first real test is getting geared up and that means you need to pick the perfect landing spot, one that's away from rivals. *Don't* jump out at the first opportunity, instead you should ride the bus a little longer and get some distance from the pack.

The eye of the storm

2 You'll want to avoid the storm at all costs. Once every player is on the ground a circle will appear on the map in a random position. If you want to have any chance of survival, you'll need to stay inside it. Over time the circle will contract, creating an ever-tighter combat zone for the remaining players. If you fall outside of this your health will start to deplete pretty quickly.

IMPROVE YOUR BUILDING

Here's how to build your way to victory

Build menu
Get your head around the build menu and you'll be creating your own awesome structures and pieces of cover in no time! Once you click the relevant button it will start building itself automatically.

Turbo Building
Head to Settings and switch on Turbo Building. This will let you seamlessly build so long as you have the resources. Just hold the crafting button down and point the cursor in the right direction.

Pre-game
In the pre-game lobby you can pull up the build menu and edit objects. The edits will stay in position throughout the game. Try editing the pyramid so that it becomes a stair-less slope.

Build under fire
As objects build automatically they can be used while in combat, providing temporary cover or the chance for you to escape. As soon as you hear a shot, start building a wall.

Be creative
While building giant towers looks cool, the best use of the building system comes into play when you're trying to cross large gaps or get up and down mountains quickly. Be creative with it.

Take your time
It's worth spending some time in the Wailing Woods. Get resources and start practicing away from other players. The more comfortable you feel, the easier it'll be under fire.

Practice your building

4 Once you've got some resources you'll want to start building. Structures can be used to get you out of trouble or utilized to provide cover and higher ground. You need to get comfortable using the Turbo Building system, so spend a few games practicing in the Wailing Woods.

Get geared up

5 *Battle Royale* is all about fighting until you're the only one left. To do that you need some gear. The map is littered with items, from long-range weapons to support items such as shield potions and bandages. You'll need to get as much of this as you can before you begin encountering players.

An eye on rarity

6 Weapons come in several varieties and rarities. Keep an eye out for anything with a colored glow. The higher tier of rarity the more powerful and useful it will be. Gray is common, green is uncommon, blue is rare, purple is epic, and orange is legendary. If you see something purple or orange grab it *at all costs*.

Pick your battles

7 Just because you've got all of this gear and resources doesn't mean you should immediately run into the first firefight you come across. It's actually surprisingly easy to get into the final 20, you just need to avoid combat wherever possible and pick your battles. Only engage another player when you're absolutely certain you can win it and try to think creatively to get out of combat scenarios.

Move swiftly and quietly

8 Everything you do in *Fortnite* will make noise, from opening doors to smashing down structures. If you want to survive *Battle Royale* you'll need to keep moving, but, you know, in a cautious fashion. Be wary of moving through open spaces, don't make noise unless you have to, and don't shoot unless you have no choice.

Watch out for other structures

9 As the player numbers begin to dwindle and the circle starts getting really tight, you'll likely notice some pretty radical player fortifications—towers and strongholds—beginning to pop up around you. You should avoid approaching them if you can, as it means another player is in there and has the higher ground. If you *do* need to attack one, try to use weapons with a high fire-rate, or explosives, and attack the base of the structure.

Embrace failure

10 Learning the basics of *Fortnite: Battle Royale* is one thing; becoming a master of it is another thing entirely. If you really want to earn yourself that Victory Royale you need to embrace failure. Try different things, get comfortable with all of the systems, and experiment with some weird tactics. Sure, it might get you killed the first time, but who knows, the next time it may just make you a legend.

DYNASTY WARRIORS 9

UNITE THE THREE KINGDOMS

The *Dynasty Warriors* **series is well known for its one-versus-a thousand combat.** Set during the Three Kingdoms period in China, you select a legendary warrior then lead the charge on the battlefield and take on the entire enemy force to help your side conquer the land. There are many characters to choose from, each with their own unique weapon, and every battle can be won in a variety of ways, giving you an excuse to go back, replay, and see if you can find a better way of winning. The latest game, *Dynasty Warriors 9*, brings an open-world environment, a first for the series. You can travel across China by foot, horse, or boat, see landmarks like the Great Wall of China, and stop at villages along the way to upgrade your equipment or buy new gear from the blacksmith and stables. History has just gotten a whole lot more fun!

STATS

87 main characters have been playable over the main series

1997 is when the first game launched on the PS1

11 Spin-off series based on *Dynasty Warriors'* mechanics

184 is the year of the first chapter

TOP 5 WARRIORS

Slug it out on the battlefield in style!

1 Lu Bu

His name strikes fear into the hearts of any soldier who hears it. Known as the "Warrior of all warriors," Lu Bu fights just so he can find someone worthy of defeating him. He enters battles by cutting through waves of soldiers on his horse, Red Hare, the fastest in all the kingdoms.

2 Guan Yu

The noble oath-brother of Liu Bei and Zhang Fei, Guan Yu is as well known for his combat skills as he was for his beard. Towering over everyone else on the battlefield, he is an intimidating sight, but for those on his side he is also a motivating commander.

5 Sun Shangxiang

One of the most popular female characters in the series, Lady Sun is known for her determination. She learned martial arts at a young age and became a skilled archer so she could fight alongside her older brothers.

3 Zhou Tai

Known as "The silent blade," no one is quicker with a sword than Zhou Tai. He barely says a word; letting his actions do all the talking. He is willing to throw himself in front of attacks to save his leader Sun Quan and he has gained many scars because of it.

4 Cao Cao

Described as fierce, ambitious, and cold, he causes those around him to fear his presence, but Cao Cao's only goal is to make the world a peaceful place. He is willing to do anything to complete his mission and that is what has taken him from a Chancellor to the founder of Wei Kingdom.

TIPS & TRICKS

Listen to allies
Your allied officers will inform you of any problems or incoming attacks; listen out for these and try to react quickly.

Look at your options
There are numerous ways of breaching castles. Battering rams, siege towers, and grappling hooks are all effective ways of getting in.

A good defense
When fighting any of the legendary warriors, don't forget to block. Wait until your opponent is weak before going in to attack them.

Gather resources
Hunting animals in the wild will get you materials for creating accessories that boost your stats, so explore when you can!

ROBLOX

MILLIONS OF GAMES IN ONE

Roblox **isn't really a game; it's somewhere you go to *play* games.** Or make one of your own games to share with the world! Available on PC, Mac, iOS, Android, and Xbox One, *Roblox* gives you access to a huge, ever-growing library of games made by other players from around the world. And all for free! Fight other players; race other players; maybe just pretend you work at a pizza place, or play around in a water park! There are so many different types of games to play and discover.

You will have to use a computer to create your own games, but playing other people's can be done on any compatible device. In fact, *Roblox* players can play together no matter what device they're using!

STATS

64 MILLION active players each month

2006 The year the Roblox platform was released

7.5 million total views of "Roblox Pizza" on the Roblox YouTube channel

29 MILLION games

FINDING THE BEST GAMES

HOME   AVATAR   GAMES   FRIENDS   ROBUX

ROBUX

Roblox really is completely free to install and play . . . but the in-game money, Robux, costs real money to buy. It can be used to buy, for example, special "VIP" status and bonuses in some games. If you want to start spending Robux, you must have an adult's help and permission.

OBLIVIOUSFERN2

FRIEND ACTIVITY

Your friends are not online

FAVORITES

RECENTLY PLAYED

FEATURED

YOUR AVATAR

Your character in the game—your avatar—is a little *Roblox* person like this. Lots of games let you temporarily change how you look, or automatically make changes for you. Sometimes, this is the game itself, such as a fashion show where your costume choices are judged by other players!

FAVORITES

With so many games to play, what about the ones you *really* like? You don't want to lose them. *Roblox* has your back! It'll keep track of your recently played games, but you can also add games to a favorites list so you can jump back in whenever you want.

FEATURED GAMES

Having more games than you could ever play is great, but what if you miss out on the best ones? *Roblox* still has your back! It'll highlight some of the best in "Featured", a regularly updated list. Try it out; you might find a new favorite . . . for your favorites list!

ALSO CHECK OUT . . .

LittleBigPlanet

Sony's cute series isn't just a collection of platformers; each game allows you to make and share your own levels or mini-movies, and play and rate the ones others have made.

Dreams

From Media Molecule—the same company that made *LittleBigPlanet*—*Dreams* offers a similar make-and-play experience, but on a much bigger scale. You can use ready-made objects to make a level in minutes!

GAMING'S COOLEST SECRETS

LOOK A LITTLE CLOSER . . .

We always think we're the ones in control in video games. Come on, who can blame us? Eventually everyone beats the main quest, or gets to the final level, or just becomes the most powerful character anyone has ever seen. But even when you think you're finished, there's a good chance that the game isn't finished with you. Because we're not always in control. In fact, hidden away in games are devious secrets included just for the sake of being difficult to find and to prove that we might not know games as well as we think . . . even if we have a level 100 stealth archer who can hear a butterfly breathing from two miles away. Here are the best secrets we've found (just to prove we are in control. Because we definitely are).

HORIZON: ZERO DAWN
Some special rabbits

Near a metal flower in the northeast of the map, you'll find two very peculiar rabbits. Sneak up on the pair when they're snuffling around on a rock, and if you scan them you can see that they're called Jazz and Jack! They're a reference to the game *Jazz Jackrabbit* from the 90s.

YOOKA-LAYLEE
Hidden controller carvings

Paying attention to anything other than staying alive during a boss fight might sound crazy, but give it a go when you're battling The Great Rampo. Look closely at him and you'll see engravings of retro gaming controllers (you will recognise them as SNES and Genesis controllers from the 80s and 90s).

CUPHEAD Turn everything black and white

Finding the Turtle
At Isle Three you'll find the Turtle, who says that pacifist platformers see the world "in shades of gray." Intriguing . . .

Complete the Pacifist quest
Now comes the tricky bit—complete every single Run 'n Gun level without killing any enemies. No, we're not joking.

See the world in monochrome
Once you're done, the entire world of *Cuphead* will turn black and white! The music even sounds more old-timey too.

MARIO KART 8 DELUXE

Change the Animal Crossing season

The Animal Crossing track has a hidden mechanism to change the season. First make sure you're offline (and not playing time trials), then tap R for Summer, L for Spring, ZR for Winter, or ZL for Fall. Match it to the current season in real life for extra immersion!

WHAT REMAINS OF EDITH FINCH

Step into the Unfished Swan

Explore Milton's room and you'll find the trademark yellow steps found in another game, *The Unfinished Swan*. Milton disappears to become the King in that game. Not convinced? Milton's cartoons depict him wearing a crown and a giant mustache, just like the King in *The Unfinished Swan* . . .

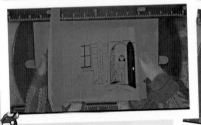

POKÉMON ULTRA SUN & ULTRA MOON

Pokémon Trainer is a gamer

Dig through your room in the Melemele Outskirts and you'll find a Nintendo Switch. Your trainer obviously enjoys playing Nintendo's latest console!

MARIO + RABBIDS KINGDOM BATTLE

Luigi's super-quick dab

After Luigi uses his Sentry to shoot an unlucky enemy, there's a chance that he'll quickly dab instead of using his usual finger gun gesture. Because he's cool like that.

THE EXPERT SAYS...
DAVID FOX
Game Designer
KNOWN FOR...
Thimbleweed Park

In our graphic adventure, *Maniac Mansion*, there's a chainsaw you could pick up, but when you look at it, it says it's out of chainsaw gas. This was a red herring since the gas doesn't exist anywhere in the game. We got a lot of flack from this, but of course a working chainsaw would ruin a bunch of puzzles (just chainsaw through a locked door). So when I did *Zak McKracken*, I added a can of chainsaw gas inside of a locker on Mars. When looked at, the character would say, "It's for a different game. Use for chainsaws only."

UNCHARTED: THE LOST LEGACY
Chloe does some yoga

In Chapter 4, climb right to the top of Hoysala Tower (you can get up there using the broken door you used to get in). Leave Chloe standing at the very top and after a while she'll start doing yoga! This will also earn you the Your Prize Trophy too.

CRASH BANDICOOT N-SANE TRILOGY
Nathan Drake's photo

Those bandicoots sure have a soft spot for *Uncharted's* charming Nathan Drake. Who can blame them? Keep an eye on the decor of the Bandicoot home, and in the background behind Crash you'll see a small portrait of Nathan Drake next to a pot of flowers, roguish smile and all.

OVERWATCH
Sombra's high score

Most people think that the Blizzard World Map has nods to every Blizzard game apart from *Overwatch*, but that's not true. In the Heroes Arcade by the door there is an electronic leaderboard with the top score being 9999 by SMB. Given Sombra is a hacker, we doubt that she got this score fairly.

ARMS
Change your character's outfit color

Bored with your favorite character's outfit? We have a solution! Press the left analog stick when you're selecting your fighter, then move the stick either up, down, left, or right at the same time. Press A simultaneously and bingo! Your character will be transformed right before your eyes.

LEGO MARVEL SUPER HEROES 2
Frozen visits New York

It's official: *Frozen* exists in all realities, even fictional video game ones. In Manhattan, if you listen closely you can hear a citizen say, "the cold never bothered me anyway." Either it's a coincidence, or they're singing along to Elsa's *Let It Go* song in their head.

THE LEGEND OF ZELDA: BREATH OF THE WILD
Find and tame Ganondorf's horse

Be in the right place
Travel to the Taobab Grassland, in the Lake region. Watch out for a giant horse with bright green eyes and orange hair.

Prepare yourself
Equip some stealth armor, and a ton of stamina-boosting elixirs. You'll need them if you want to tame the horse . . .

Time to tame!
Master Ganondorf's steed by sneaking up on it then jumping on its back. Drink stamina elixirs until it stops bucking!

SPLATOON 2
Be the DJ

Change the lobby music to your liking by pressing X, Y, B, and A to add warped voice lines, and make them sound high-pitched or ominously deep by moving the left analog stick around. Warning: they do sound a bit creepy at times (maybe don't play with this part in the dark).

AWESOME CAMEOS

The Legend of Zelda: Breath of the Wild

CAMEO STAR Satoru Iwata (Nintendo's former CEO)

Travel to the Outskirt stable in Hyrule Field to find Botrick patrolling the nearby road. Botrick's appearance is a tribute to Satoru Iwata, Nintendo's CEO, who passed away in 2015.

Rayman Legends
CAMEO STAR
Prince of Persia

In the Nintendo Switch version, you can dress up as the Prince of Persia right away. Rayman's outfit references Ubisoft's swashbuckling Prince who lives in . . . yup, you guessed it. Persia.

Super Mario Odyssey
CAMEO STAR
Yoshi in Mushroom Kingdom

Throw Cappy onto the scarecrow behind Peach's Castle to get onto the roof. Run to the front to find the spotty egg that Yoshi is hiding in!

NIDHOGG 2
Hidden Donkeyspace achievement

To get this sneaky hidden achievement, you simply have to play a game for over 20 minutes. Yes, that sounds rather difficult. But it doesn't necessarily mean you have to have an intense duel with someone for quite that long (thankfully). Set the game rules to make sure the time limit is either 20 minutes or "NONE". Then just keep *Nidhogg 2* open until the achievement pops! You can do this either on local co-op or online, and you don't even have to fight to get it and instead let your very squishy fencer have some well-deserved rest.

Pokémon Ultra Sun and Moon
CAMEO STAR
Dexio and Sina from *Pokémon X and Y*

Have a look around Heahea City, and you'll find Professor Sycamore's assistants Dexio and Sina on their own little holiday. Plus they give you the Zygarde Cube!

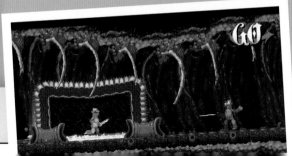

TOP 5 SUPER MARIO ODYSSEY SECRETS

A bird for every occasion

2 Leave Mario alone for too long and he'll take a nap. Before you disturb his slumber, wait a little and a bird will land on his nose! It changes depending where you are, from a penguin in the Snow Kingdom to a bird with a top hat in Cap Kingdom.

Donkey Kong's city

1 The entirety of New Donk City is—surprise surprise—a reference to the barrel-throwing Donkey Kong. Streets are named after characters from the series like K. Rool and Expresso, plus Diddy's Mart refers to Donkey Kong's nephew Diddy Kong, and Squawk's Park is named after one of Kong's animal buddies. That's bananas!

Getting into the Odyssey

3 Most people use the front door when they enter their high-tech ship/airplane hybrid. Not Mario! He can also enter the Odyssey through the exhaust pipe at the back by crouching, or through a roof hatch. We think they're emergency entrances in case he locks himself out. Nobody's perfect.

THE EXPERT SAYS...

JON ECKERSLEY

Senior Principal Artist at Media Molecule

In *Zelda: Link's Awakening*, which I played as a kid, in the village shop, you pick up an item before taking it over to the shopkeeper to pay for it. However, if you run around him in circles, you can exit without paying—he doesn't quite keep up with where you are. If you re-enter the shop later, he immediately kills you with a lightning blast! All the characters in the game will now refer to you as THIEF.

Cactus payday

4 Hit a round cactus with your hat, and it'll give you one coin. Big deal. But if you manage to hit multiple cactuses one after the other, at the end you'll get a mountain of coins (and by a mountain we mean eight).

Moon hands

5 When Mario gets himself a moon, watch his hand closely. He'll have different hand gestures that match the ones he used in previous games! There's a peace sign from *Mario 64*, a fist from *Mario Galaxy*, or an open palm from *Mario Sunshine*. All that's missing is a thumbs up . . .

THE SIMS 4
Left or right-handed Sims

Look closely at your Sim of choice when they're gardening, or painting, or cooking. Notice anything? That's right, each Sim is either left or right-handed! Just like us real people, Sims prefer doing their activities with their dominant hand. Their preference is randomly generated when they're created. Neat.

INJUSTICE 2
Superman is super-arrested

Pick a fight between Batman and Superman, and you'll spot a sly reference to the first *Injustice* game. Batman will mutter that Superman belongs in jail, which is a nod to the first game where —SPOILERS!—Superman ends up in prison at the end. Where're some kryptonite handcuffs when you need them?

SONIC MANIA
A slogan from the past

When you reach the Studiopolis 2 level, you can flip some of the letters to make them spell all sorts of things. They might look like a random jumble of letters, but persist and they'll eventually spell out "Welcome to the next level," one of Sega's slogans from the 90s.

OKAMI HD
Force people to pet Ammy

You can make Ammy's canine dreams come true with one trick. All dogs love to be petted, after all. Draw the Bloom symbol around people and they'll run towards Ammy to pet her! If you're too far away, they'll sulk. Ammy's fur is probably soft, so we don't blame them.

DID YOU SEE THAT?!

CUPHEAD

The first two bosses of *Cuphead* aren't easy, but their attack patterns are basic and easy to remember. Hilda Berg is the first boss to really test you, and it is also the first boss to be fought in the airplane. The key to beating any boss is to never stop firing your weapon and to focus on dodging. Like a lot of other battles, there are small enemies that can catch you off guard, and you should also watch for the bosses signaling their attacks.

1 Hilda's first form is pretty simple; she will fly up and down, occasionally shooting a projectile. Just stay to the left-hand side of the screen, moving up and down with Hilda. Make sure you take out the small, purple blimps as well.

2 The boss will eventually inflate and rush towards you. Stay at the top or bottom of the screen until she re-enters as a bull. Hilda's only attack in this form is stretching towards you but after a short amount of time she transforms back to the unicycle form.

3 The next form of Hilda is random as it can be one of two things; twins that spin and drop an orb firing bullets in a circle, or an archer who shoots arrows that fire stars at you. To dodge either of these attacks, fly in a clockwise or counter-clockwise direction.

4 Hilda's final form is a giant moon taking up almost half of the screen. Stars will fly towards you and UFOs will pass above. Gold UFOs shoot in a pattern while red UFOs only shoot when you're under them. Just keep dodging and firing, then eventually you will win!

Biscuit
60

Flapper
75

Ariel
100

Crumpet
60

Rowan Boat
60

DID YOU KNOW?

You can unlock hats from games like *Yooka-Laylee*, and even use weapons like a car from *Rocket League*!

WORMS

TINY CHARACTERS, HUGE EXPLOSIONS!

Want to take on your friends in a tactical game of worm-based war? Of course you do! The *Worms* series has been around since 1995 when the first title appeared. The latest release, called *Worms W.M.D*, returns to the classic gameplay of the original, but with some fun twists. For a start, you can now join in with up to five others in a match, and when each player has four worms on their team, that's a lot of targets to aim for! You'll have plenty of tools to use, too—there are dozens of new weapons, including some from other games like *Rocket League*. And, because the game is now available on Nintendo Switch (as well as Xbox One and PS4) you can take the explosive invertebrate action with you wherever you go.

The Sheep & The Worm

STATS

Bomb icon by 23 icons

There are

22 🎮
mainline *Worms* games

60+
weapons to use

70,000,000
Worms games sold and downloaded

UP TO

48 worms
per multiplayer match

TOP 5 WEAPONS

ARMAGEDDON

1 If you've had enough of your opponents, this is the tool to use. Armageddon summons a barrage of meteors that fall from the sky and cause explosions all over the stage! There might not be much left of the stage when the meteors stop, though . . .

ATTACK HELICOPTER

2 This flying menace can be used to travel across the stage and do damage to other worms while you go. If you find one on the battlefield and jump in, you can zoom up and over other worms, fire down on them below, and then land somewhere far away from them to avoid retaliation.

TANK

3 *Worms W.M.D* added tanks to the maps, allowing any worm that can reach them to jump in and roll around. The tank's main gun causes quite an explosion and its armor will also protect your worm a little, giving your little guy a big advantage.

CONCRETE DONKEY

4 This bizarre weapon is unstoppable. Call it in and, well . . . a concrete donkey will fall from the sky. What else were you expecting?! It bounces as it falls, causing explosions with every impact, and it keeps bouncing and exploding until it reaches the bottom of the stage and sinks. It causes a lot of damage, but to be honest you'll be laughing too much to notice!

BANANA BOMB

5 This hilarious explosive has been a staple of the series since the very first game in 1995. Throw this innocent-looking fruit and it will explode after a few seconds, sending out smaller banana shards. These shards are also very explosive, and can do massive damage if they land in the right place!

TIPS & TRICKS

Watch for mines
These explosives are dotted around on the floor and can be hard to spot. Keep your eyes open!

Save your weapons
Don't use a cool weapon as soon as it unlocks—save it until you really need it later to do some big damage.

Go up high
Taking the high ground is always a good idea. It makes you harder to hit, and lets you reach more areas with weapons.

Take cover
There are buildings dotted around some levels that can provide good cover from weapons. Don't be afraid to hide!

NI NO KUNI II: REVENANT KINGDOM

VISIT A MAGICAL REALM

DID YOU KNOW?

Evan's surname, Tildrum, is shared with the cat king from the first game, set hundreds of years earlier.

At the beginning of *Ni No Kuni II,* a young king called Evan has his kingdom stolen from him by the leader of a rival tribe of rats. Playing as Evan and the gang of friends he gathers around him, your quest is to win his magical kingdom back. You get to explore a huge, colorful cartoon-world, accompanied by memorable characters like the daughter of the air pirates' boss, Tani, and Roland, a man who has magically appeared from another world. You can switch between different characters when fighting monsters to use their different abilities and can harness the magic of cute little creatures called Higgledies that will fight alongside you. Higgledies are also useful when you're exploring the world. Their special elemental powers—like wind and fire—can be used to access new areas that you can't get to otherwise.

STATS

SPECIAL SWORD DLC brings new weapons **5**

Special Collector's Edition limited to **25,000** units

3 Editions of the game: Standard, Premium, and Collector's

Runs at **60** fps

TOP 5 BITS OF MAGIC

Breaking down what makes *Ni No Kuni* special

THE HIGGLEDIES

3 Who doesn't love those cute little Higgledies? They add an interesting layer to the game's battle system with their cool elemental powers and help you to access new areas in the world with their unique powers. Oh, and did we mention they're cute?

THE CHARACTERS

1 Though *Ni No Kuni II* doesn't follow on from the first game directly in terms of story, it's certainly followed on when it comes to delivering great characters. The people and creatures you meet in this game are full of personality and often have something funny to say.

EPIC SCALE

4 *Ni No Kuni II* feels epic in more ways than one. First there's the size: it's a massive place full of charming villages, dry deserts, lush forests, and much more. Then there's the fact that its story involves a whole kingdom, a visitor from another world, and a personal tale of growing up.

SKIRMISH MODE

5 *Ni No Kuni II* adds a new mode that isn't in the first game called Skirmish mode. It's a strategy-like battle mode where you control a small army of characters and command them to help you conquer new territory.

STUNNING STYLE

2 You only need to take a quick look at this game to see that one of the things that makes it special is its style. Studio Ghibli, creators of classic films like *Spirited Away*, helped create the art style for the first game and those amazing visuals have been improved for the sequel.

TIPS & TRICKS

Use your Higgledies

Don't forget about your Higgledies when you are battling. Their elemental powers are important in helping you win.

Stun enemies

If you need to stun your enemy to buy some time, you can order your Higgledies to leap on their back.

Come back later

Some areas can't be accessed without the right Higgledies, so just come back later if you get stuck.

Switch your troops

In Skirmish mode, make sure you are using the color of Higgledie that is strong against the color of troops you are fighting.

TOP 10 SPEEDRUNS

Longest Star Wars speedrun
LEGO Star Wars: The Complete Saga

1 The longest solo *Star Wars* world record stands at a massive 13 hours, 22 minutes, and 13 seconds. Zulice accomplished the run on the Nintendo Wii version of LEGO *Star Wars: The Complete Saga*, which required him to complete all six in-game episodes on multiple occasions as he sought a 100 percent completion rating. Strong with the Force, this speedrunner is.

The cooperative speedrun
Portal 2

2 The multiplayer mode in puzzle-platform game *Portal 2* requires players to work together to solve a range of complex challenges. This is exactly what speedrunners Zypeh and AJ managed to achieve—the pair completed the mode in a super-quick 28 minutes and 25 seconds. It's a truly impressive run, featuring a mix of clever tricks, dizzying skills, and, most importantly, brilliant teamwork.

Entering the Nether
Minecraft

3 In order to reach *Minecraft's* ending, players are tasked with traveling to the Nether and slaying the all-powerful Ender Dragon. This quest is seemingly designed to take hours, but even without the aid of glitches, TheeSizzler managed to complete it in a record seven minutes and 12 seconds. By using additional tricks, he also went on to finish the run in less than five minutes.

SIX TIPS TO BE A GREAT SPEEDRUNNER

1 CHOOSE YOUR GAME WISELY
In order to speedrun a game you'll need to learn it inside-out. Be sure to pick something you enjoy, as you'll be spending a lot of time with it!

2 STUDY OTHER PLAYERS' RUNS
You'll find other players' speedruns and their tutorial guides online. With these, you can learn tricks to help you complete quick runs.

3 LEARN FROM YOUR MISTAKES
You're bound to make errors along the way, but don't worry! Making mistakes is part of the process, and you can learn some valuable lessons!

4 PRACTICE, PRACTICE, PRACTICE!
To speedrun a game, you'll need to practice it loads. To start, focus on finishing the game. Then practice the bits you struggle with.

5 STAY CALM & HAVE FUN
Speedrunning can be a frustrating hobby when things aren't going your way. Remember to stay calm and take regular breaks!

6 DON'T AIM FOR WORLD RECORDS
Many runners will tell you that speedrunning isn't about achieving world records. Instead, focus on trying to beat your own times!

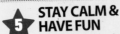

The blindfold challenge
Mike Tyson's Punch-Out!!

4 This game sees you fighting to face Mike Tyson in the ultimate showdown. It's a hard game to beat, but add a blindfold and that challenge becomes almost impossible. mPap is one of a few players to have defied those odds, finishing the game in just 20 minutes and 27 seconds while blindfolded.

The blistering speedrun
Sonic Generations

5 *Generations* is one of the best games in *Sonic's* catalog, with both classic and modern-style levels across nine stages. Its runs are blisteringly fast, with thebluemania's current world record standing at 53 minutes and 41 seconds.

The gnarly run
Tony Hawk's Pro Skater 2

6 It's easy to spend hours in *Tony Hawk's Pro Skater* without ever completing the main campaign. Amazingly, speedrunner guished required just two minutes and 56 seconds to conquer the series' second outing, blasting through each of the game's eight levels in record time.

An unlikely feat
Pokémon Snap

7 This game is all about taking pictures of your favorite Pokémon. It's more concerned with capturing photos than finishing as quickly as possible, but speedrunners have found ways to improve their times. The current record is held by quo, who finished the game in just 20 minutes and 50 seconds.

THE EXPERT SAYS ...
DARBIAN
Former *Super Mario Bros.* World Record Holder

When you're looking to get into speedrunning, most people struggle to choose their first game. There are many different criteria in a speedgame that each person will weigh differently, so there isn't any blanket rule that will apply to everyone. I recommend just choosing a game you enjoy playing and seeing how it goes. You are not locked into your decision and can change games whenever you like. You'll have a much better idea of what you want in a speedgame after actually trying one. The most important factor is whether or not you're having fun. Forcing yourself to do something you don't enjoy will never work out, and at worst might turn you off of a hobby you may otherwise have really enjoyed.

The shortest speedrun
Clue: Murder at Boddy Mansion

8 The US edition of this virtual board game has become notorious for its speedruns. By guessing the correct suspect, weapon, and room, it's possible to complete *Clue* in less than a second. The record for the game is held by i_o_l and stands at an astonishing 0.633 seconds.

The expert speedrun
Cuphead

9 With its super-difficult bosses and challenging gameplay, *Cuphead* has been a huge hit with speedrunners. The current record, held by luigi100, for defeating all the game's main bosses on Expert difficulty is an impressive 27 minutes and two seconds.

The best speedrun ever
Super Mario Bros.

10 Nintendo classic *Super Mario Bros.* is one of the most popular games for speedrunning, and record-holder Kosmic has consistently impressed with his completion times. His current record stands at four minutes, 56 seconds, and 462ms!

All records correct at the time of going to press.

EPIC HAIR, EPIC FIGHTS

DRAGON BALL FIGHTERZ

Japanese anime doesn't get bigger than *Dragon Ball Z.* The larger-than-life characters and OTT action makes it perfect for games, but only now do we have a fighting game that can be counted among the greats like *Street Fighter.*

Dragon Ball FighterZ looks and feels like you're playing a cartoon, but the characters and stages are actually 3-D, and everything runs super smoothly. It's pure tech magic! It's also chaotic, with up to six fighters zipping in and out of the action, unleashing screen-filling super moves. But don't worry, with special moves and combos made easy, you can focus on mixing and matching your team for the ultimate brawl.

Whether or not you're a *Dragon Ball* fan, this is a beautiful fighting game to sink your teeth into.

STATS

24 PLAYABLE CHARACTERS to choose from

3 playable arcs in story mode

Extend combos to over **100** HITS!

The **44**th DRAGON BALL GAME released on console—not even including on handheld/mobile

SUPER SAIYAN SET-UP

TRIPLE TROUBLE

The game is designed as 3v3, so you always pick a team of three fighters. They can be swapped in and out of battle with a button press, or use assist moves. When playing online, you can even have a team of three players controlling individual fighters. Team communication is vital!

SEEING GOKU

Dragon Ball's huge cast of characters includes alternate timelines that also feature in the game. Take lead protagonist Goku (also playable in his Super Saiyan Blue form): here he's not actually fighting himself but Goku Black, a villain from another timeline, who has his own special moveset.

CHANGE OF PERSPECTIVE

It looks like a 2-D fighter now and most of the action stays fixed with side-on view. But when you perform the high-level super moves, the camera changes, showing your fighter recreate their signature attacks straight out of the TV series—all beautifully rendered in-engine.

METER MADNESS

Crazy super moves use up your super gauge, which you can have up to seven stocks of meter. While other fighting games usually fill this up based on the damage you dish out or receive, you can also just build it up manually by holding the "Ki Charge" button.

ALSO CHECK OUT . . .

Guilty Gear Xrd
Can't get enough of anime fighters? This was the first *Guilty Gear* game that made the technical leap from animating hand-drawn sprites to cel-shaded 3-D models, which *FighterZ* also uses.

Marvel Vs. Capcom: Infinite
While the art style may differ from *Dragon Ball FighterZ*, *Marvel Vs. Capcom: Infinite* combines your favorite characters from the Marvel and Capcom universes with an insanely fun fighting game.

PREPARE FOR A CUTENESS OVERLOAD
OOBLETS

Look at them, just *look at them.* Actually, don't look directly at them for too long: you could fall victim to a cuteness overload. These little critters are the Ooblets, and they were lovingly created by indie dev duo Rebecca Cordingley and Ben Wasser for their debut game *Ooblets*. This brilliant life simulator/monster battler/farming game combines the likes of *Pokémon* with *Animal Crossing* and *Stardew Valley*, and wraps it all

up in an adorable art style that even the coldest, darkest human being is certain to fall in love with. *Ooblets* is set on a familiar, yet outlandish, planet called Oob, and you have to grow your cute critters from the ground, like sentient screaming potatoes. Then, you can set off and battle them against one another. Now, if that's not enough to convince you on this breakout hit, we don't know what will.

STATS

2 DEVELOPERS MADE IT

559 patrons on Patreon

37,000 views on its debut trailer on YouTube

31 DIFFERENT OOBLETS

TOP 5 OOBLETS!

Get to know these strange alien vegetable beings

PANTSABEAR

1 Let that name sink in for a second: *Pants-a-bear*, it's literally a bear in a pair of pants. Excellent. One of the more grizzly critters from *Ooblets'* roster of strange animals, Pantsabear has the qualities you'd expect from a bear, like claws . . . only, he's wearing pants.

SHRUMBO

2 Kind of like how Pikachu captures everything good about *Pokémon*, Shrumbo is *Ooblets* in a nutshell: cute, looks like it comes from the ground, and, err, cute again. Shrumbo is, obviously, based on a mushroom, so expect it to have some spore-related attacks.

DID YOU KNOW?

All of the awesome artwork in the game is done by Rebecca Cordingley and then Ben Wasser handles the overall game design.

BRISTLEBUD

3 For when you need a friend with some bristles, call on Bristlebud. This ooblet looks to be based on everyone's favorite low-maintenance plant: a cactus. Its spines will prove handy if you choose to send it out into battle. On the flipside, though, Bristlebud can't really be cuddled. How sad.

CLICKYCLAWS

5 We're not quite sure *what* Clickyclaws is, to be honest. Part-flower, part-alien, part-grumpy Monday morning, Clickyclaws likes to use its sharp nails to attack other Ooblets. It's pretty notable that this creature is one of the few Ooblets to actually deal damage in the game's reveal trailer.

RADLAD

4 Another ooblet that we're classing in the "definitely-looks-like-some-radioactive-waste-dripped-on-a-vegetable" category, Radlad is, well, a rad little radish with a pair of long legs. Okay, we'll level with you: he's only on the list because he's got "rad" in his name.

ALSO CHECK OUT . . .

Pokémon Ultra Sun & Ultra Moon

The most famous monster-battler on this planet, basically everyone has heard of *Pokémon*, and for good reason: it's excellent in every way and its most recent generation is fantastic.

Animal Crossing New Leaf

For those of you who prefer the idea of farming and making friends, look no further than *Animal Crossing*. This cute little life simulator keeps you hooked and brings a little bit of light into your everyday life.

OKAMI HD

A TRUE MASTERPIECE

It might have been released over a decade ago, but *Okami* is back, and more beautiful than ever. The classic adventure game has been revitalized for PC, Xbox One, and PS4, and stars the fearsome Amaterasu, a white wolf who also just happens to be goddess of the sun. Armed with the Celestial Brush, a magical item that lets you paint things to life on the game's canvas, it's up to you to bring peace back to a land overrun with dragons, demons, and other dangerous foes.

Inspired by Japanese folklore, *Okami* is filled with charming characters and breathtaking locales that take advantage of its gorgeous visual style. Don't be surprised if you spend some time just admiring the scenery as you breathe life back into Nippon—it is like playing a painting come to life.

STATS

88 Metascore on Metacritic

15 weapons to earn and equip

Over **30** awards won

100 STRAY BEADS TO COLLECT TO ASSEMBLE A HOLY ARTIFACT

TOP 5 CELESTIAL BRUSH TECHNIQUES
Master these brushstrokes and start painting with power

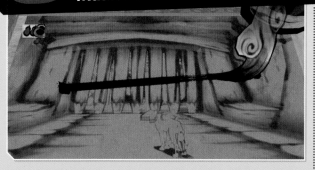

POWER SLASH

1 One of the earliest techniques you'll acquire in *Okami* is also among the most useful. Whether chopping down barriers to access new areas, or going head-to-head with your enemies in the heat of battle, you will find all sorts of uses for Power Slash throughout your adventure in Nippon.

GALESTORM

4 Once obtained from the wind god Kazegami, this stroke becomes invaluable. Its uses range from extinguishing dangerous fires to accessing new areas by propelling lily pads across water. And the winds summoned by Galestorm can even knock flying demons out of the sky, ready for Amaterasu to finish them off on the ground.

BLOOM

2 Another versatile technique, Bloom is the first of the 'Greensprout' strokes acquired from the trio of monkey gods called the Hanagami. Bringing cursed trees back to life and making flowers sprout might not seem like the deadliest of skills, but just try using it on a Bud Ogre in battle!

INFERNO

3 Inferno is exactly what it sounds like, a stroke that can conjure scorching flames that burn down flammable barriers and incinerate enemies. This technique is bestowed upon you by Moegami, the god of flames, a flying rooster who smokes a giant, flaming pipe.

VEIL OF MIST

5 Amaterasu is pretty nimble as wolf deities go, but sometimes even she needs to move more quickly. That's where Veil of Mist comes in. This handy technique slows the flow of time for a short period, during which you can dodge fast-moving obstacles or land a flurry of hits on an enemy.

ALSO CHECK OUT . . .

The Legend of Zelda: Breath of the Wild
A sprawling adventure filled with memorable characters, monstrous enemies, and spectacular set pieces.

Ni No Kuni II: Revenant Kingdom
Okami's style is unique, but there are other RPGs out there that are just as stunning in their own way. The Studio Ghibli-inspired graphics of *Ni No Kuni II* make it a treat to watch and play.

DID YOU KNOW?

PS4 player Hakoom has the record for most Trophies. He has over 1,200 Platinums!

HARDEST ACHIEVEMENTS

We've put together a collection of the toughest Trophies and Achievements you can earn in the world of gaming. Getting them will be a real test, but when you see that Trophy or Achievement pop, you'll have the satisfaction of knowing you're one of the elite few to have it. With our expert tips on how to beat these tough challenges and unlock the rarest of gaming achievements, we'll guide you to gaming greatness.

20

SONIC MANIA
(PS4, Xbox One, Switch, PC)

Professional Hedgehog

To unlock this Achievement or Trophy you need to get through Act 1 of Titanic Monarch Zone without taking any damage. Pick Tails, as his flying ability means you can fly back where you came from if you mistime any jumps. Take it slowly and be very cautious.

19

THE ESCAPISTS 2
(PS4, Xbox One, Switch, PC)

I Am Your Father

Select the U.S.S. Anomaly stage with a friend and raise your intellect to 70. Get four batteries, four wires, and two broom handles. Craft two energy modules with the batteries and wires, then combine them with broom handles to make energy swords. Hand one to your buddy and fight for the achievement.

18

FIFA 18
(PS4, Xbox One, Switch, PC)

Fake it Make it

Perform a fake shot to trick the keeper, then score with a finesse shot. The keeper has to dive at your feet for the achievement to count. Press shoot, followed by X on PS4 or A on Xbox One to perform a fake shot. Round the keeper, hold R1 on PS4 or RB on Xbox One and shoot to score a finesse shot.

17

CUPHEAD
(Xbox One, PC)

Pacifist

You need to complete all the game's levels without killing any enemies to be awarded this Achievement. We recommend buying the Smoke Bomb charm from Porkrind's shop to help with this. You won't take any damage while dashing with it equipped, allowing you to dash through hazards and enemies.

16

STEAMWORLD DIG 2
(PS4, Switch, PC)

Solid Sneak

You have to make your way through Vectron without triggering more than two alarms to get this one. A couple of alarms are unavoidable, but for the rest, you can dig your way under or quickly leap over the alarm triggering robots before they are alerted and start hunting you down.

15 FOOTBALL MANAGER 2018 (PC)

Immovable Object

Not conceding a single goal in 30 games is a near-impossible feat, but it can be done. Pick a strong team in a division that's not too competitive. Set defensive tactics, but don't be *too* cautious against weaker teams where you can control possession and stop them having the ball.

14 FORZA MOTORSPORT 7 (Xbox One, PC)

Underdog

Sometimes there's no shortcut to getting an achievement—you just have to get good. That's the case for this Achievement where you must start a 24-player multiplayer race last and finish first. You're just going to have to practice until you're good at the game and get a bit of luck.

13 PUYO PUYO TETRIS (PS4, Xbox One, Switch)

Prismatic Popper

You need to eliminate four different colors in one move to unlock this achievement. Set your handicap to Medium or Spicy then set your Puyos up in a stack so that when you eliminate the bottom row, the correct colors will drop down and match up.

12 THUMPER (PS4, Xbox One, Switch, PC)

All S Rank

When chasing S ranks on every stage to get this achievement, don't worry about getting perfect turns, as these impact your score, not your rank. You must hit every note and not take any damage to get an S rank. Restarting from a checkpoint won't impact your rank, so retry as much as you need to.

11 RIME (PS4, Xbox One, PC, Switch)

Hold Your Breath

In Chapter 3 you'll come across some underwater caves. Get through them using only one bubble and you'll be rewarded with an achievement. The only cave you need to use a bubble in is the second one. Take the fourth bubble you come across and you can just make it.

10 — EVERYBODY'S GOLF
(PS4)

Absolute Finesse

You need to score a hole in one on a 5-par course to unlock this Trophy. You'll want upgraded clubs at power level 20, a triple precision ball, and a control stat of 15 on your driver. Alpine Forest Open Course Hole 12 is your best bet for making this tough shot.

9 — CITIES: SKYLINES
(PS4, Xbox One, PC)

Tough City

You need your city to survive with a 40 per cent crime rate for two years for this achievement. Build a small city with only fire and garbage services and crime will start climbing. If the crime rate goes too high, zone more residential to bring it down.

8 — HOLLOW KNIGHT
(PC, Switch)

Steel Soul

You must finish the game in Steel Soul mode—that means you can't die once! Use Fragile Charms for this run as the penalty of them breaking on death doesn't apply. If you're about to die, you can cheat a bit by quitting to the menu and then reloading.

DID YOU KNOW?

The World of Nubla offers one of the quickest and easiest Platinum Trophies on PS4—achievable in around two hours.

7 — SNAKE PASS
(PS4, Xbox One, Switch, PC)

No Diving

To complete Lazy Lagoon without touching the water and unlock this achievement, you'll need to be well practiced at controlling the snake. Stick to the water's edge, wrap yourself around bamboo, and climb up walls to stay dry.

6 — MARVEL VS. CAPCOM INFINITE
(PS4, Xbox One, Switch, PC)

Solo Round

Dominate an online opponent so much that you defeat them without switching partners, and you'll be rewarded with this achievement. Head into Training Mode and perfect your combos with your best character. Once you're ready, it's just a matter of taking your finely tuned skills online.

TOP 5 EASIEST ACHIEVEMENTS

Enter the Ruins
Undertale (PS4, PC)
You enter the ruins right at the beginning of *Undertale*. There's no challenge in the way. All you need to do is play for a few minutes and you'll have this Trophy.

Let's play a game
FIFA 18 (PS4, Xbox One, Switch, PC)
A shockingly rare achievement, given how easy it is to get. All you need to do is play a women's soccer match. Simple.

Ring Pull
Full Throttle Remastered (PS4, PC)
You get this for solving the game's first puzzle. After the barman refuses to give you any info on your missing keys, use the hand icon on him.

Welcome To Just Dance 2018!
Just Dance 2018! (PS4, Xbox One, Switch, PC)
All you need to do to unlock this achievement is complete one song. You don't need a good score or anything like that—you just need to finish it.

Operation: Rebirth
LEGO Marvel Superheroes 2 (PS4, Xbox One, Switch, PC)
After completing the game's second mission, you will unlock a character creator. All you have to do to get this achievement is use it to create your own hero.

5

MLB THE SHOW 17
(PS4)

Straight Flexin'
You must hit a home run that travels 430 feet in Retro Mode for this one. Pick an All-Star team and put your power hitters in the starting line-up. Set the hitting difficulty to Beginner. Now just keep swinging until you nail it and send the ball flying.

4

MICRO MACHINES WORLD SERIES
(PS4, Xbox One, Switch, PC)

Aggressive Gardener
You need to be playing on The Mighty Mower stage in Online Battle to get this achievement by pushing five opponents into the lawnmower in one battle. Captain Smallbeard is the best choice of vehicle for this one thanks to its handy push ability.

3 PARAPPA THE RAPPER REMASTERED
(PS4)

Comeback King

To earn this Trophy, you need to come back from an Awful rating and end with a Cool one. Simply miss the beats at the beginning of the level until you're rated Awful, then turn on your rhythm-action skills and push your score up before the song ends.

THE EXPERT SAYS ...
XEINOK
The most Steam achievements

Achievement hunting is a hardcore community in gaming where the goal is to complete as many games and challenges as possible. Achievements started as GamerScore reward points for challenges in Xbox games, but now achievements are also on PlayStation and Steam. If you ever played a game where you just felt like you had to collect everything and beat every level, you would probably love achievement hunting because that's what hunters do for every video game they touch! Achievements bring a lot of extra replayability and challenge into games, so you really get your money's worth by 100%ing them.

2 STREET FIGHTER V
(PS4, PC)

Back From Hell

You need to beat Survival Mode on Extreme for this Trophy—that's 100 fights with one bar of health! Use your points to buy health boosts between rounds when possible. If you're struggling, try picking Ken, and spamming his Dragon Punch!

1 DESTINY 2
(PS4, Xbox One, PC)

The Prestige

To complete the Leviathan raid on Prestige difficulty and earn this Achievement or Trophy, it goes without saying that you should practice the raid on normal difficulty first. It's a good idea to have one of each class in your team to give you as many options as possible and that you should all be packing high-level gear. You need to rush through as much as possible to beat the tight time limit, so only kill enemies you need to and revive your teammates rather than relying on self-revives, which take far too long.

1 Is there a tricky jump in your way? Well Funky Kong can double-jump to get some extra height. Not only that, but when in the air Funky can also use his surfboard to hover, allowing you to reach that little bit further along.

2 The bosses you fight in *Tropical Freeze* are known for taking a lot of hits, and dealing lots of damage. But unlike other characters, who take either two or three-hit points before dying, Funky can take five! His hit points are shown in the top-left corner.

DID YOU SEE THAT?!

DONKEY KONG COUNTRY: TROPICAL FREEZE

While it is lots of fun, *Tropical Freeze* is also incredibly hard. Tight jumps, aggressive enemies, and numerous obstacles will get in your way. So when the game got ported over to the Nintendo Switch, the developers added a new mode to help get beginners accustomed to it. In Funky Mode you get access to Funky Kong, who, thanks to his surfing skills, has some unique abilities to get through the aforementioned obstacles. Let's check out these cool new abilities . . .

3 There's absolutely no need to worry about slowing down when you hit the water as the cool Kong can spin infinitely using his corkscrew maneuver. Funky also doesn't have an air meter, so you don't need to worry about reaching the surface before dying.

4 Anyone who has played a lot of platformers will know the feeling of dread that you get when you see a pit full of spikes. But do not fear, as perhaps Funky's best ability is useful here. He can use his surfboard to avoid getting damaged by spikes or thorns.

KNACK 2
BITS AND PIECES OF AWESOMENESS

Attention all evil monsters and sinister robots: *Knack* is back, so get ready to battle and brawl! In this exciting sequel to the original PS4 title, you control the same hodgepodge hero from the first game, only with way more abilities to unlock and even crazier enemies to fight. The Goblins have returned and are terrorizing everything and everyone, so it's up to Knack and friends to put an end to the chaos. What's cool about the main character in this game is that since he's made up of thousands of ancient, magical pieces called relics, he can shrink to the size of an action figure or grow to the size of a building—all at the press of a button. Smash, jump, dash, and dodge your way through 15 beautiful chapters of platform-action goodness.

STATS

The first *Knack* came out in

2013

as a PS4 launch title

Knack can add

5,000

relics to his body

Knack 2 took

3 years to develop

2 people can play through the game in co-op mode

THE MISHMASH WARRIOR

OOOOO! AHHHHH!

Knack 2 is one beautiful game, but PS4 Pro makes it look even better. There are two main options: you can choose to have ultra high-res visuals that show off crisp textures, or go with a super high frame rate to make the game run faster. Either way, those magic relics have never been more shiny.

BFFs

Returning in *Knack 2* is a new and improved co-op mode, which means that you and a buddy can play through the whole game together as separate red and blue Knacks. You can combine powers to unleash insane combo attacks, and really, nothing says true friendship like teaming up to smack down some Goblins!

BUFFER IS BETTER

Knack 2 is much better than the original, and one of the biggest improvements is combat. As you defeat enemies, you'll earn relic energy that can be used to purchase different upgrades, like the Super Dodge, the Somersault Kick, and the Hook Shot. You'll be a Goblin-smashing machine in no time!

TO-DO LIST

Even after you finish all 15 chapters, *Knack 2* still has plenty left to do. There are time trials to complete, harder difficulties to conquer and treasure chests to track down. If you collect enough Crystal Relics you can unlock one of four Crystal Knacks, super cool skins that give your hero some amazing powers.

ALSO CHECK OUT . . .

Super Lucky's Tale

Take on the role of an adorable fox and defeat the evil Jinx in this colorful 3-D platformer. You can tail swipe enemies, dig around underground, and collect special clovers that unlock new levels.

A Hat in Time

The main objective in this goofy platforming adventure is to wear as many hats as possible and return home. Control Hat Kid as she collects hour glasses and extra yarn for knitting ability-granting headpieces.

ROCKET LEAGUE

ROCKET-POWERED SOCCER ACTION!

How do you like the sound of rocket-powered cars flying around an arena at high speed, trying to knock a giant ball into a goal? Awesome, right? Well that's *Rocket League*. The game pits you and your friends against an opposing team, and the aim is to score more goals than them! It's a bit like soccer, except you can explode opposition players by driving into them at top speed, giving you a short advantage until they respawn. The game is now available on Nintendo Switch, meaning you can play anywhere, or give your friend a Joy-Con controller and play in the same room. Sitting next to your teammates while you play makes it even more fun!

STATS

48 vehicles to unlock or purchase

30 MILLION registered players

21 million views on *Rocket League* **YouTube** channel

OVER 10.5 MILLION COPIES SOLD

TOP 5 GAME TYPES
Mix up your matches!

HOOPS

1 This basketball-inspired arena has a large hoop at each end. In order to score you need to hit the ball up into the air so that it drops through the hole. But with six rocket-powered cars knocking the ball around, it's much harder than it sounds!

SQUARE BALL

2 You can add all kinds of "Mutators" to a *Rocket League* match, and one of them is to make the ball a little less round! The cube shape will make the bounces of the ball hard to predict, so everything is a little bit tougher. You'll need luck on your side to win.

ROCKET LABS

5 To try something a little different, why not take a trip to Rocket Labs? These arenas are all totally different from the standard rectangular field. Some have more than one goal for each match, while others add different levels or other obstacles to the area.

DROPSHOT

3 Your team needs to protect its side of the arena in this game mode. If the ball bounces on your side while charged up, it will damage the floor and the ground will start to disappear beneath your tires! Destroy the other team's floor and knock the ball through it to win.

HOCKEY PUCK

4 Want a more slippery way to play? Try swapping the ball out for a hockey puck and watch as it zips across the arena floor. Hit it hard enough and it will zoom up the wall, or start flipping over, making it incredibly difficult to stop!

TIPS & TRICKS

Have a goalie
One member of your team should stay near your goal to defend against incoming shots. It might win you the game!

Learn to fly
Point your car upwards, hit boost and you'll fly! This is really useful for reaching bouncing balls.

Get boosts
Make sure you're driving over the boost pads as often as possible—having a full boost bar is vital to reaching the ball first.

Front-flip for speed
If you're out of boost but want more speed, jump and then do a front flip. It gives you a mini boost!

Block
You don't have to hit the ball. If you see an opponent going for the ball, drive into them to block their shot!

DID YOU KNOW?

Pikmin are named by Captain Olimar after a type of carrot on his home planet, known as "Pikipik".

FLOWER POWER ON THE GO

HEY! PIKMIN

The *Pikmin* series has always been about **downsizing—shrinking you down to discover the microscopic world that the colorful critters inhabit.** And in *Hey! Pikmin*, Nintendo has taken that idea even further by moving the series to a handheld console.

Here you once again don the spacesuit of Captain Olimar and enlist the help of your pint-sized Pikmin pals to recharge your broken-down spaceship. To do that you need Sparklium, and to get Sparklium you'll need to scour the 2-D levels for hidden items. A snowglobe, an old battery, and a discarded NES cartridge might not seem like the best rocket fuel, but a human's trash can be a diminutive alien's treasure.

Olimar can't do it alone, but with some petal-headed Pikmin to clear obstacles, solve puzzles, and take down enemies, anything is possible.

STATS

30,000 **Sparklium** required to fuel the **S.S. Dolphin II**

9 SECTORS **TO EXPLORE**

57 KINDS OF ENEMY CREATURE TO DEFEAT

32 **SECRET LOCATIONS** THAT CAN BE **UNLOCKED** WITH DIFFERENT **AMIIBO**

TOP 5 PIKMIN TYPES

There's a Pikmin for every occasion

RED PIKMIN

1 These fiery fellows can handle heat and flames without batting an eye. If you find yourself blocked by a pit of flames, simply throw a group of Red Pikmin in and they'll quickly douse the blaze. They also have above-average strength, so they are a good bet for taking down your enemies.

YELLOW PIKMIN

2 These Pikmin are always worth a place in your party. They're lighter than normal, so can be thrown up to hard-to-reach platforms, and they're resistant to electricity too, so won't get fried like some of your other Pikmin. They can even open locked doors by conducting electric currents through their bodies.

BLUE PIKMIN

3 Captain Olimar's spacesuit means he can venture underwater any time—but the same can't be said for most Pikmin. Luckily, Blue Pikmin have gills that let them breathe while submerged, so they can accompany you into watery environments in search of any sunken pieces of treasure.

WINGED PIKMIN

4 After first appearing in *Pikmin 3*, Winged Pikmin return to help you navigate some of the game's more hazardous levels. They can lift Olimar up to help him over chasms too wide to cross with his jetpack alone, and they can also raise up some barriers blocking your way.

ROCK PIKMIN

5 Not only are these boulder-like companions the strongest Pikmin around, making short work of all but the toughest enemies, they're crucial to accessing certain areas as well. If you find your path blocked by a large crystal, try flinging some of your Rock Pikmin at it. Smash, bang, boom—and you're through!

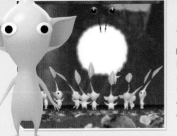

ALSO CHECK OUT...

Metroid: Samus Returns

If you're looking for a bit more of a challenge after finishing *Hey! Pikmin*, then this could be the answer. It offers the same side-scrolling platforming, but with added alien-blasting action.

Rayman Legends

A classic platformer that's now available on Nintendo Switch, *Legends* is filled with stunning environments and crazy critters, not to mention all the secret areas and collectibles that you can seek out and discover.

TOP 10 VR GAMES

Minecraft Gear VR

1 How could it not be? Using Samsung's Gear VR, you can actually play *Minecraft* in full VR—something so many of us have dreamed of for so long! It's the full game with every feature enabled, so you already know the game itself is brilliant, but the addition of your newfound perspective makes it like entering the world of *Minecraft* all over again for the first time. Just watch out for (VR) Creepers!

Echo Arena

2 It can get a bit intense, but you are playing 5v5 futuristic robotic Frisbee in *Echo Arena*, and Frisbee in real life gets intense too! What makes *Echo Arena* special, aside from it being great fun, is how it allows up to five people to spectate on the match you're playing, meaning you can have a real crowd watching and cheering you on!

Lone Echo

3 The partner game with *Echo Arena* is *Lone Echo*, a single-player story you play through located in a mining facility in the rings of Saturn. VR is the only way you'll get to go there, after all! With clever problem solving and in-depth dialogue, *Lone Echo* is easily one of the best games on Oculus Rift and up there with the best in all of VR.

6 TIPS TO GET YOURSELF VR READY

EASE YOURSELF IN
Don't expect to go from no VR to 12-hour sessions in one day. You have to train your brain to get into virtual reality. Take your time and soon you'll be an actual, virtual expert.

MODIFY THINGS
You can always change options to suit what you're comfortable with in VR games, whether that's changing how the camera moves or how you control the game.

TAKE REGULAR BREAKS
This advice tends to get ignored when playing "regular" games, but it's something you should pay attention to. Take breaks. Have time away from the headset.

CHOOSE GAMES CAREFULLY
Oculus marks its games with a comfort rating, so check that out on its site to see how uncomfortable a game might make you feel. It's all about finding the level for you.

DRINK WATER
It seems odd to give this bit of advice for playing games, but a sip of water every now and then can help a lot if you're feeling queasy. Just try not to knock the glass over!

TAKE THE HEADSET OFF
If, even after training yourself, you feel uncomfortable playing a VR game, just take the headset off! Nothing's stopping you, and it will help you feel better, faster.

Star Trek Bridge Crew

4 Who hasn't wanted to be the captain of the Enterprise? Or the science officer? Or just an ensign? *Bridge Crew* lets us all live out these dreams, playing with friends in a team to run a Federation Starship on missions and boldly go where no one has gone before.

Robo Recall

5 *Robo Recall* features you battling a robot army. Who wouldn't want to do that? It's intense and engaging, and you get to feel like a real superhero as you take on the metallic armies of the opposition. With Oculus's touch controller, it's even more convincing.

Superhot VR

7 Time pauses when you're not moving in *Superhot VR*, meaning you have the chance to plan your next moves. While this would make most other games really easy, here you're always outnumbered and nearly overwhelmed, so the chance to stop and plan what to do is helpful. The fact that you're right there in the action when you start moving and the fight begins is great.

Project Cars 2

8 *Project Cars 2* is a "standard" game for the most part, but an update was released to allow VR compatibility—and we're glad it was. This is a great driving simulator, and being right there in the car as you hurtle around a track at hundreds of miles an hour is an exciting experience, just as if you're driving in a real-life Grand Prix race. Just make sure that you take breaks every now and then!

Psychonauts in the Rhombus of Ruin

10 It's not the longest of VR experiences, but this spin-off from *Psychonauts* is beautiful and very funny—and who wouldn't want that in their reality (which is virtual?). It also works as fan service for those of us who love the original platformer series.

Gnog

6 You might not expect that you'd want to look at monster heads in VR, but *Gnog* proves everyone wrong. It's a tactile puzzle game in which you discover the secret worlds hidden inside those monster heads we just mentioned, and it's as crazy as it is fun. Because there's little moving around, it's really accessible for players of all ability levels too—a great VR title.

Infinite Minigolf

9 It's not a pure VR game, but *Infinite Minigolf* manages to be fun, endlessly replayable (infinite courses!), and something that really suits being played in VR. You remain still while taking your shot, giving you a better look at the course in proper 3-D. So even if it's not specifically a VR game, *Infinite Minigolf* is definitely great fun in VR.

DID YOU KNOW?

Six of the voice actors involved in *Xenoblade Chronicles 2* have also lent their vocal talents to the *Thomas The Tank Engine* TV show.

XENOBLADE CHRONICLES 2

AN EPIC SWITCH-BLADE ADVENTURE

Everything about *Xenoblade Chronicles 2* is massive. From the sprawling sci-fi storyline, to the dozens of different features and wrinkles of the battle system, this isn't an adventure you dip into casually. Even the environments you travel through are set on the backs of Titans—creatures so huge that entire countries have been founded on them!

If you're looking for an RPG to get lost in, then this is it. *XC2* stars a young hero called Rex who, along with his Blade companion Pyra, sets out in search of Elysium. Blades are both characters and magical weapons, and they play a big part in the game's combat. Upgrading Blades is key to taking down enemies, and you'll assemble a collection on your way to getting Rex and Pyra to their goal.

STATS

85 HOURS — time of average playthrough on howlongtobeat.com

39 rare and special Blades to collect

8 major Titans in the world of *Xenoblade Chronicles 2*

7 main games in the Xeno meta-series

TOP 5 BLADES
Much more than just weapons

PYRA

1 One of the most prominent characters in *Xenoblade Chronicles 2* and Rex's primary companion throughout the game, Pyra is a Blade of phenomenal power. Her fiery elemental abilities make her a formidable ally on the battlefield, but they're also why she's wanted by some of the world's most dangerous villains.

FINCH

2 One of the more unusual Blades in *Xenoblade Chronicles 2*, Finch is a bird-like creature who wields a wind-powered hammer. Though she's on the forgetful side, she always gives her all in battle, and while she might not look like it, she can soak up a lot of damage.

FLOREN

3 Having a healer in your party is really important in *Xenoblade Chronicles 2* and Floren is one of the best around. His healing battle skills include "Blossomfall" and "The Coming of Spring."

WULFRIC

4 If there's a scarier Blade than Wulfric then we haven't found it. He strikes with a huge lance that deals serious elemental damage. When activated, his battle skills can increase the potency of your attacks.

AZAMI

5 She may act shy and helpless, but Azami is anything but. Her dark elemental attacks mean she's a great Blade for when you want to take the fight to the enemy.

ALSO CHECK OUT . . .

Final Fantasy XV
After years in development, the epic 15th installment in Square Enix's flagship series didn't disappoint. If you haven't yet joined Noctis and his crew on their road trip for the ages, you absolutely should.

Bravely Second: End Layer
A traditional Japanese RPG, *Bravely Second* might not bring much innovation to the table, but it makes up for it with its intriguing world, well-told story and enjoyable turn-based combat system.

GAME SERIES

DROPMIX
R-R-R-REMIX!

DropMix **is what happens when you combine a card game, a video game, and tons of great music.** So how do you jam to this DJ-style interactive mixing experience? Download the free app, pair your mobile device with the cool electronic board (which lights up, by the way), and choose from one of three heart-thumping game modes: Clash, Party, and Freestyle. This is where the NFC-enabled cards come in.

As you place a card on the board, it unlocks and plays a part of a popular song. This can be drums, vocals, or a funky bass line. That part keeps playing as the next card is added, and every new card brings another ingredient to the mix. You can choose from lots of music, like Bruno Mars' *24K Magic* or Ed Sheeran's *Sing*.

STATS

COMES WITH 60 NFC music cards

5 cards can be used simultaneously on the board

Up to **5 PEOPLE** can play *DropMix*

ONE *DropMix* button to smash

FREESTYLE
DROP THE BEAT

HEAD-TO-HEAD

Clash is *DropMix's* classic versus game mode in which players face off against each other in a battle of music and strategy. The main goal here is to get 21 points before your opponents, all by dropping cards into the mix and spinning the Equalizer to clear the other team's hand.

TOTAL FREEDOM

The Freestyle game mode is a great place for *DropMix* newbies to start. Anything goes in this music free-for-all, so place cards on the board randomly or in any combination you choose. Once you're done, you can save your best mix and share it with friends over the internet.

GET THIS PARTY STARTED!

In Party mode, there's only one team and everyone's on it. Here it's all about what the crowd wants, so you and up to four friends need to pay attention to the music requests and place the correct cards on the board as fast as possible. Can you get the highest score?

SWEET TECH

DropMix uses something called NFC (near-field communication), the same technology that makes *Skylanders* and LEGO *Dimensions* work. Inside each music card is a small chip that the game board wirelessly recognizes. That information gets sent to your mobile device, which then starts playing the correct song. It's like magic!

ALSO CHECK OUT . . .

Guitar Hero Live

This modern *Guitar Hero* reboot is everything you loved about the previous games, only now there's real people (actors, actually) cheering in the audience and playing music with you on stage.

Aaero

One part on-rails shooter, another part dubstep simulator, *Aaero* has you taking control of a futuristic spaceship, doing battle with a giant sand worm, and blasting one huge glowing spider. Also, the soundtrack is amazing.

DID YOU KNOW?

Click on the logo of the developer ConcernedApe during the loading screen and the sunglasses will come off, accompanied by a honk sound.

STARDEW VALLEY

CREAM OF THE CROP

An indie farm simulation RPG, *Stardew Valley* actually began life as a *Harvest Moon* fan game. But four years of development later and it's undeniably in a world of its own, and has become one of the best-selling titles on Steam, with its pixel art-style, quaint environments, quirky townspeople, and satisfying quests. *Stardew Valley* takes the best of all of its inspirations and ties it all together in one neat little package, including the farm and general story themes of *Harvest Moon*, crafting and dungeon exploring of *Minecraft*, friendships and fishing of *Animal Crossing*, and much more. There are so many different things to do in *Stardew Valley*, in fact, that every person playing it is likely to have their own goals. Will you become a farming fanatic? Or an explorer extraordinaire? The richest resident? Or a creative cook? It's up to you!

STATS

71 RECIPES TO COOK

1 person, Eric "ConcernedApe" Barone, developed the entire game

Current record for deepest floor reached in the Skull Cavern **525**

1,000,000 THE COST OF THE MOST EXPENSIVE ITEM: THE STATUE OF ENDLESS FORTUNE

TOP 5 WAYS TO MAKE MONEY

Time to make the most of those cash crops

BOUNTIFUL FRUIT

1 Some crops are more worthwhile to farm than others—blueberries, for example. One blueberry plant will net you 70g after selling its first three fruits from the first harvest. But because it keeps on producing and there's a chance that it could grow more than three blueberries, you can end up earning a lot more than you think!

LOOK FOR LEGENDS

2 Legendary fish are worth more money than your normal catch of the day. Try fixing the bridge by Elliott's house on the beach, going across to the east and fishing off the end of the Pier to have a go at catching Crimsonfish! It's worth 2,250g!

GO FOR GOLD

3 Once you've discovered the mine after the fifth day, you can dig for rocks—unearthing ladders to progress downwards. The further you go, the better the treasure, and if you can find enough gold ores, you can smelt them into gold bars to sell on. You'll be rolling in cash in no time.

ARTISAN

4 Make a processing machine, then create a Preserves Jar to turn normal fruit and vegetables into pickles and jellies worth twice their normal price. Alternatively, create a Mayonnaise Machine to turn eggs into delicious mayo worth almost four times their original value.

TRACK THE TRAVELING CART

5 The cart will appear south of the farm in Cindersap Forest every Friday and Sunday. Buy a Rare Seed from there and grow it for 24 days in the Fall. It'll bear a Sweet Gem Berry worth 3,000g.

TIPS & TRICKS

Stairway to heaven
You can explore the mine faster by building staircases out of stones. You can save space by only building them when you need them.

Recipes for success
You can collect a different recipe every Wednesday and Sunday on the TV by watching *The Queen of Sauce.*

Saved by the Rail
Stuck at the mine and it's already midnight? Hop on the Rail Cart to go straight to the Bus Stop next to your farm and you'll be home in no time.

Effortless fertilizer
You can use any fish to make the Quality Fertilizer, so save time, money, and effort by using what appears in the Crab Pot!

Quicker quests
You can complete some of the Community Center quests faster by keeping an eye on the rarer items that are being randomly sold at the Traveling Cart.

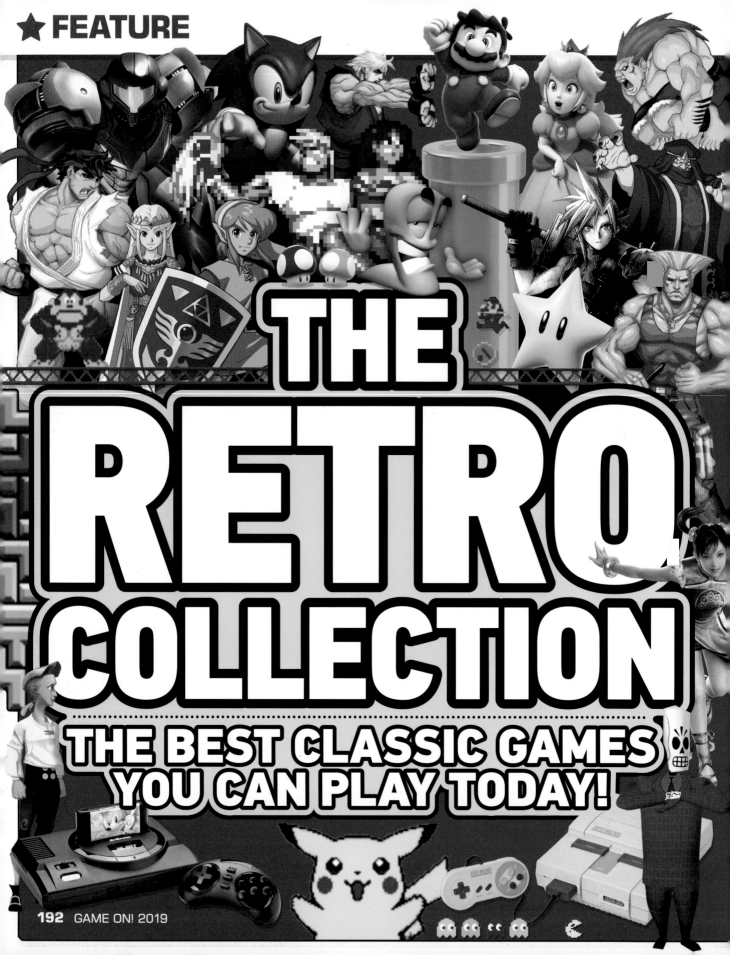

THE RETRO COLLECTION

THE BEST CLASSIC GAMES YOU CAN PLAY TODAY!

It can be tempting to only care about the newest games out there—but older, retro titles can be fun to play too! Not only that, they can be a great way of learning about the games you know and love today, by showing how your favorite series and characters came to be. But above all they're a lot of fun. So, with that in mind, we've decided to bring together some of the best retro games around. They might not have the shiny graphics of today's games, but we think you'll love them all the same!

PONG
Just search "Pong" in your browser

20 One of the most well-known old games is *Pong*. It's as simple as they come, with a bat on either side of the screen, each trying to get a ball past the other. You'd be surprised, then, at just how much fun it can be to play against a friend even now, many years after it first came out.

POKÉMON RED AND BLUE
Nintendo 3DS eShop

19 *Pokémon* continues to grow and grow, but you shouldn't ignore where it came from—and the first couple of releases in the series are still great fun to play. Journey back to when there were only 151 pocket monsters out there and catch 'em all!

STREETS OF RAGE 2
Nintendo 3DS eShop, iOS, Android, Steam, PlayStation Store

17 Scrolling beat-'em-ups were all the, ahem, rage back in the 80s and 90s, and few show off this style of game better than *Streets of Rage 2* for the Sega Genesis. Grab a friend and play through this one, we guarantee you'll have a load of fun—and the music is great too!

THE SECRET OF MONKEY ISLAND
Steam, Xbox Live, PlayStation Store, iOS

18 Point-and-click adventure games had been around for a while before *Monkey Island* arrived, but it was the first game to perfect the formula. It's also still one of the funniest games ever made and has a real *Pirates of the Caribbean* vibe. It's well worth your time!

SONIC THE HEDGEHOG 2
3DS eShop, iOS, Android, Steam

16 One of the best games on Genesis is still vibrant, beautiful, and fun to this day. Playing *Sonic 2* is a brilliant way to see just why the blue blur is loved by so many. Modern *Sonic* games may have seen the hedgehog with attitude lose some of his magic, so going back to this classic of the series is definitely worth your time.

DONKEY KONG
3DS eShop, Wii U eShop

15 Mario's first appearance in gaming might not be exactly what you'd expect, but *Donkey Kong* is still a great game in its own right. You simply have to get from the bottom of the screen to the top, avoiding barrels and flames as you go. Simple? Sure. Easy? Nope. This is a challenge for the ages!

SUPER MARIO KART **3DS eShop, Wii U eShop**

14 The original game in the *Mario Kart* series might have aged when it comes to looks—though we still love it—but it still plays as well as it ever did. Play against a friend and you'll quickly see why this is one of the definitive multiplayer games of all time.

TONY HAWK'S PRO SKATER 2
iOS, PS3 backwards compatibility

13 The game that defined the youth of many kids in the early 2000s, *Tony Hawk's 2* is a masterclass in skating action, with a killer soundtrack. It's all about scoring as many points as possible (and finding some hidden secrets), and it's as compelling and fun today as it was almost 20 years ago.

WORMS **Steam, various other versions**

12 Four friends, all-out turn-based warfare, random levels, explosive sheep. Oh, also everyone involved is a worm. One of the true greats of multiplayer gaming, *Worms* has been updated—and improved—many times over the years, but it's always fun to go back to the very first and see how things were back in the mid 90s.

DEDICATED RETRO MACHINES

SNES Classic Mini

Nintendo's follow-up to the NES Mini is a superb (and very) little machine, with 21 built-in games, including the never-before released *Starfox 2*. It looks amazing, plays everything perfectly and adds in some modern features like the ability to save at any point and rewind to help get past the more difficult parts of a game. It is the gold standard for dedicated retro machines and worth every dollar.

KEY GAMES **Super Mario World • The Legend of Zelda: A Link to the Past • Super Metroid**

Sega Genesis Flashback HD

Admittedly this isn't as good as Nintendo's own Classic Mini, but the miniaturized Genesis option on the market is good enough. With 45 Genesis games and additional Master System and Game Gear titles thrown in for good measure, there's plenty to keep you playing for a while. Not every game included is a bona fide classic, and there are some issues with emulation, but one bonus is that it plays original Genesis cartridges, in case you have some in the attic!

KEY GAMES **Sonic the Hedgehog 2 • Alien Storm • Phantasy Star IV**

Retron 5

This specially made retro machine accepts original cartridges for a number of different consoles: the SNES, Genesis, Game Boy, Game Boy Advance, and more. As such, it's a really cool gadget to have that lets you play all of those classic games you might be able to find in a flea market on your modern TV! It also plays games from other areas of the world, like Japan and Europe, so you can even pick up titles that never released in the United States.

KEY GAMES **Super Mario Bros • Pokémon Red and Blue • Advance Wars**

PC and Steam

When you're thinking about retro gaming, you shouldn't overlook the PC or Mac you have at home. These machines aren't strictly dedicated to retro gaming, but there's more than enough out there on Steam (and other digital stores) to let you pick up and play some of gaming's greats. You'll find classics from tons of different computers and consoles. Just look at the Genesis collection on Steam—dozens of Sega titles, all there on your PC!

KEY GAMES **Almost anything!**

THE BEST OF NEW RETRO
COOL NEW GAMES INSPIRED BY THE CLASSICS

Hyper Light Drifter

This game pays homage to the likes of *A Link to the Past* and as such it has some big shoes to fill. Fortunately it's brilliant, emulating the classics of the 90s with a visual style all its own.

Stardew Valley

Farming might seem like a boring way to spend your gaming time, but *Stardew Valley* gets it right. You'll soon be getting involved with crop placement and the welfare of your livestock.

Terraria

The 2-D alternative to *Minecraft* has a graphical style that takes us back to the 16-bit era. Build grand and crazy structures as you try to survive in an unforgiving, hostile land.

Shovel Knight

Taking inspiration from classics like *Mega Man*, *Shovel Knight* brings us platforming combat action with a hefty dose of difficulty. It looks the part, it plays the part, and it's super fun too!

Super Mario Odyssey

Mario's latest adventure is full of nods to the original *Super Mario Bros.*, *Mario 64*, and many more. Best of all, none of it feels like it was put in without thought—it all fits, and it's all brilliant.

MS. PAC-MAN
iOS, Android, PS3, Xbox 360, Steam

11 The first *Pac-Man* might be the one most folks remember, but we have to throw our lot in with the follow-up—*Ms. Pac-Man* and her bow. It's a more refined version of the maze-running, ghost-avoiding, cherry-chomping arcade classic, and it's more than enough fun to play even to this day.

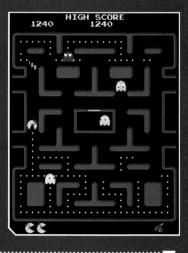

SPACE INVADERS
iOS, various other versions

10 When you talk about arcade games, you have to talk about *Space Invaders*—and when you talk about it, you probably want to play it, and when you *play* it, you realize it's still brilliant fun. Just remember to always shoot up through your own bases. It makes sense when you play!

STREET FIGHTER II TURBO: HYPER FIGHTING
SNES Mini, iOS, Android

9 *Street Fighter II* changed fighting games forever, but it was *Turbo* that hit the high point for the series. Fortunately *Hyper Fighting* still holds its own to this day, easily standing alongside the latest game in the series and managing to offer a whole load of fun of its own.

GRIM FANDANGO REMASTERED
PlayStation Store, Steam, iOS, Android

8 A true classic of the adventure genre, few games can match the epic story, mind-bending puzzles, brilliant humor, and fantastic musical score offered in *Grim Fandango*. You can now experience it in all its remastered glory, so you've got no excuses for missing out.

SUPER MARIO 64
Wii U eShop, Nintendo DS

7 There were 3-D platformers before *Super Mario 64*, but none of them were anywhere near as good as Nintendo's classic. Without this, we wouldn't have *Super Mario Odyssey*, Nintendo's latest big hit, which itself pays tribute to this original. Find a way to play it, because you deserve to.

> "SUPER METROID EXPECTS YOU TO EXPLORE, BACKTRACK, AND EXPERIMENT"

SUPER METROID
SNES Mini, 3DS eShop

6 2-D graphics rarely looked better than they did in *Super Metroid*, and handily the game itself holds up to modern scrutiny too. Far deeper than you might imagine for a title released in 1994, *Super Metroid* expects you to explore, backtrack, and experiment with your weapons. It's tough, but still superb.

DID YOU KNOW?
Samus has been known to take some long breaks. 2017's *Metroid: Samus Returns* for 3DS was the first release in the series for seven years.

TEKKEN 3
PSone disc on PS3

5 This is cheating a bit, as it's harder to get *Tekken 3* than any other game on this list. If you can't find an original disc, settle for *Tekken 2* on the PlayStation Store. If you can, play *Tekken 3* because it remains one of the best 3-D fighting games ever made and a real challenge to master.

TETRIS
Steam, PS4, Xbox One, Switch

4 The classic puzzler and one of the purest forms of fun you can have in gaming, *Tetris* has been made and re-made dozens of times over the years. It's always the same concept—fit blocks to make a row, try not to let them fill your screen. And it's always just as much fun as it ever was.

THE LEGEND OF ZELDA: A LINK TO THE PAST
SNES Mini, Wii U eShop, 3DS eShop

3 One of Nintendo's best ever games might have been bettered—arguably—by *Breath of the Wild* on the Switch, but *A Link to the Past* is still worth playing in these modern times. It's always going to be a wonderful, engaging adventure, and the breadth of imagination on show is never short of astounding.

FINAL FANTASY VII
PS4, Steam, iOS, Android

2 One of the greatest RPGs of all time and a must-play for anyone interested in the history of the genre. *Final Fantasy* is one of the most well-established brands around the world these days, but that wasn't always the case. We have *Final Fantasy VII* to thank for blowing the series up outside of Japan.

> Restores MP by 100

NAME		HP	MP	LIMIT	TIM...
Potion	: 3				
Ether	: 1				
Phoenix Down	: 1				

"A MUST-PLAY FOR ANYONE INTERESTED IN THE GENRE"

DID YOU KNOW?

Final Fantasy VII was originally planned for release on the Nintendo 64, but technical limitations meant it eventually moved to Sony's PlayStation.

SUPER MARIO WORLD

© 1990,1991 Nintendo

SUPER MARIO WORLD SNES Mini, 3DS eShop

1 Simply put, this is one of the greatest games ever made. Originally released all the way back in 1990, *Super Mario World* has never been bettered as a 2-D platformer, and set in motion the development of *Mario* games as we know them today. Special mention goes to the original *Super Mario Bros.* titles, but it's *Mario World* that has best stood the test of time. The mixture of imaginative levels, creative powers, riding Yoshi, and multiplayer aspects mean it's still fun to play today. If you pick up a SNES Classic Mini you're bound to be playing this one for many, many hours.

1 As the game starts Link is awoken by a light. He wakes to find himself in an emptying pool in a large chamber. If you look around the room all you will find is a large door and a pedestal with something on it.

2 Collect the Sheikah Slate from the pedestal to open the door. This will be your go-to tool throughout the adventure, displaying your map. By collecting Runes you can give it more abilities. Go through the next door to find treasure chests containing your clothes.

DID YOU SEE THAT?!

THE LEGEND OF ZELDA: BREATH OF THE WILD

The Legend of Zelda **games are known for their expansive worlds.** Seeing a mountain in the distance and reaching it only to find a new landmark to go to is part of what makes *Breath of the Wild* so much fun. The reveal of the world has been a major part of *Zelda* games since way back in *Ocarina of Time*. While *Breath of the Wild* made some big changes to the series, it kept this key part as memorable as ever.

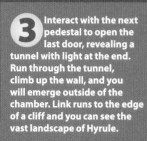

3 Interact with the next pedestal to open the last door, revealing a tunnel with light at the end. Run through the tunnel, climb up the wall, and you will emerge outside of the chamber. Link runs to the edge of a cliff and you can see the vast landscape of Hyrule.

4 From the top of the cliff, you turn right and head down the mountain. Your first encounter will be a mysterious bearded figure by a campfire who can offer advice if you need it. But after talking to him you can explore the world and your adventure can begin.

SUPER LUCKY'S TALE

JUMP FOR JOY!

Meet Lucky, the latest hero in town, who is here to help his sister rescue the mysterious Book of Ages from the villainous cat Jinx. The evil mastermind wants to reshape the world, and it's up to Lucky to stop him! As you embark on this journey you'll meet plenty of colorful characters, explore some incredible locations, and solve some tough puzzles in order to progress.

And with so much to do, thank goodness Lucky has a few tricks up his sleeve! Our foxy hero can double-jump, swing his tail to attack, and even burrow under the ground to dig up hidden coins and other secrets. The worlds you explore look fantastic, and are even more stunning if you're playing on an Xbox One X, as the game supports 4K! However you choose to play, though, you're sure to have a blast in this classic platformer.

STATS

350,000 views on announcement video

99 Clovers to collect

4 CHAPTERS TO EXPLORE

23 ACHIEVEMENTS TO UNLOCK

TOP 5 BOSSES
Fearsome feline foes

JINX

1 The leader of the gang known as the Kitty Litter, Jinx is a fearsome opponent. He can summon rings that will deal you damage, fire beams from his eyes, and make mazes that you'll need to escape from. Defeat him and you really are super!

MASTER MITTENS

2 When you enter the Dojo of Danger, you know things are going to be tough. Master Mittens makes you dodge fireballs as she summons enemies for you to defeat. Time your jumps and aim for her when you do a swipe attack to take her down.

THE MILITARY MOGGIES

3 General Buttons and Colonel Fluffy are in charge of a pirate ship, and waste no time putting it to use! Watch out for the fireballs that will cover the stage, and don't stand still for too long—unless you want Colonel Fluffy to squash you! Taking these two down is a real challenge.

TESS THE TINKERER

4 Watch out! Tess the Tinkerer has made a giant, spider-like robot and she's going to use it! You'll need to dodge her laser attacks and avoid fireballs to survive. Meanwhile, flick the switches that appear around the edges of the stage to deal Tess damage and defeat her!

LADY MEOWMALADE

5 Unlike the other bosses, Lady Meowmalade doesn't like to get her paws dirty. Rather than fight, she challenges Lucky to a tough platforming section! You'll need to avoid the obstacles and save the town's residents in order to complete the level.

TIPS & TRICKS

Look everywhere
There are hidden goodies all over the place—hit things with your tail to find secret coins, burrow holes, and many more secret treats.

Collect the clovers
There are four clovers to unlock in each level, and you'll need them to reach the final boss, so go back if you've missed some!

Stall jump
Lucky can double-jump, but if you want to hang in the air just a little longer, do a swipe attack.

Get up high
There are plenty of hidden coins hidden on high platforms! Explore as much as you can to find ways up.

Collect lives
If you're running low on lives for Lucky, revisit an easier level a few times to collect more life tokens to keep you going!

PICROSS S
FILL IN THE BLANKS

Picross **is a series that has been around for over 20 years, starting with the original Game Boy.** The puzzles in the game are known as nonograms—logic puzzles that started in Japan during the 1980s. Squares in a grid are colored or left blank based on the numbers on the sides of the grid, and when completed, a picture is revealed. Nintendo took this idea and called them picture crosswords, or *Picross*. For those who have never completed one, it can take a lot of educated guesses to get right. To help you learn the logical steps to work out the answers, *Picross S* has a simple tutorial, and if you need that little bit of extra assistance, there are hint features, too. Once you get the hang of it, you'll be finishing puzzles and feeling smarter in no time!

STATS

300 Puzzles to solve in *Picross S*

1995 when Nintendo published the first *Picross* game

17 *Picross* games Nintendo has published

500k copies of *Picross e* sold on the Nintendo 3DS

TWO-PLAY PICROSS

COLOR-COORDINATION

In two-player mode, one person colors the squares blue while the other fills in red. The menu in the top-left corner tells you who has filled in the most. So even though you are working together, there can be a competitive side if you want.

YOUR GUIDE

These numbers tell you how many squares in that row or column need to be filled in. Don't just focus on what squares are meant to be filled in—finding out which ones are meant to be blank is just as important. Use the Marker tool to indicate which squares should be left blank.

A HELPING HAND

There are three different hint systems. One will fill in a random line for you, one will highlight which rows are incorrect, and the other will correct one wrong square. If you complete a puzzle without using any of these, you will get bonus points and bragging rights.

TOP TIP

The best way to start each puzzle is to find the row or column with the highest number. Alternatively, cross out any lines that have no squares to be filled in. Beginning by eliminating the most obvious options can really help with the rest of the puzzle.

ALSO CHECK OUT . . .

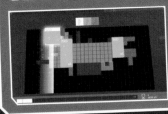

Chime Sharp

This music-based game also uses a grid, but in *Chime Sharp* you place *Tetris*-like blocks to change how the song sounds. The more of the board you end up covering, the higher the score multipliers.

Human Resource Machine

This logic-based puzzle game focuses on coding, but without all the 1s and 0s. Organize a series of commands in order to create an instruction for your worker and complete a process.

MARVEL VS. CAPCOM: INFINITE

WHEN WORLDS COLLIDE, FISTS FLY!

Have you ever wondered who would win in a fight between Ryu and Captain America? Perhaps you'd like to see the mean, green, fighting machines Gamora and Hulk team up to take on Thanos and Ultron? Then this is the game for you! The Marvel and Capcom universes have been forced together again, and this time the Infinity Stones are in the mix to give fighters special powers. Play the story mode to find out just what Ultron is up to, who's helping him, and what part heroes and villains from both universes play. Sharpen your skills in the tutorials, then go head-to-head against a friend. Or maybe take the fight online, and show the world exactly what you can do! Just remember; don't be a Thor loser. Being friendly is mega, man.

STATS

6 INFINITY STONES TO CHOOSE FROM

30 PLAYABLE CHARACTERS

2 CHARACTERS PER TEAM

5 characters new to the series

TOP 5 CHARACTERS

Choose your fighters wisely

1 GHOST RIDER

This hothead doesn't just look cool; he's a great choice for beginners and experts alike. Those chains offer good reach and speed, and do you think he'd make an appearance without his signature motorbike? Of course not! One of his special moves sees him use his ride as a weapon.

2 ULTRON

For the first time in the series, you get to play as Ultron. The bad guy who started all the trouble in the first place, threatening two entire universes at once means he has more than just the Avengers after him. But heck, being bad has never felt so good!

3 HULK

Everybody loves Hulk, don't they? If you don't, better not tell him. That wouldn't end well for you. How do you think he gets away with that haircut? Anyway, he's deadly up close, but has a few tricks to catch you out from afar, too. Hulk smash from various distances!

4 FIREBRAND

Taking time out from hassling Arthur in Capcom's *Ghosts 'n Goblins*, Firebrand is here to fight an even wider variety of enemies. Beware of any projectiles from the ground. However, who wouldn't want to play as a character who can breathe fire, right?

5 CHUN-LI

Bringing years of experience from the *Street Fighter* series, Chun-Li is an excellent addition to anybody's team. Her trademark Spinning Bird Kick can punish anybody who gets too close, while her Kikoken fireball move means opponents can't feel comfortable even when further away. A good all-rounder that shouldn't be underestimated.

TIPS & TRICKS

Using the Time Stone
Going into battle with somebody weak at a distance on your team? Use the Time Stone to teleport up close.

Using the Soul Stone
A good choice for those still learning the game, this stone's Infinity Storm will bring a teammate back to life!

Choose your team carefully
Always go for a balanced team. For example, try choosing one slow character and one fast character to switch between.

Blocking is important
Blocking up-close attacks is a good idea. The stronger the attack, the more likely your opponent will be left completely vulnerable!

Practice before going online
The online modes are full of players who have improved their skills offline, so it's worth you doing the same!

DID YOU KNOW?

Nintendo went through many wild ideas to reboot the new *Zelda*, including a sci-fi story with an alien invasion!

Breath of fresh air

The Legend of Zelda: Breath of the Wild

1 Most *Zelda* games begin with our hero Link sleeping. But this time, he awakens to a Hyrule more beautiful and vast than we've ever known. It's amazing how all the mountains and forests we see before us can be reached. Even more amazing is how after the opening hours, we'll have been given all the tools we need to explore Hyrule however we want.

Proving of an outcast

Horizon Zero Dawn

2 A future where humans have returned to tribal living while robots roam in the wild is a fascinating concept. However, it decides to focus on the personal story of Aloy, an outcast who just wants to find out who her mother is. Borrowing from classic films like *The Lion King*, we get an impressive origin of a new gaming heroine.

TOP 10 OPENINGS

6 TIPS TO LEARN WHEN YOU START A NEW GAME

1 WHAT'S THE DEAL?
Money makes the world go round. It could be coins or a collectible, but many games will have some kind of currency, whether it's to get better items or unlock new areas or abilities.

2 LOOK FOR THE HIGHEST VANTAGE POINT
In open-world games, look for the tallest structure. Climb to the top and take in the view of where to explore next. Just be careful!

3 LOOK OUT FOR THE SHINE
Game objects you can interact with or pick up are usually shiny and stick out. In other cases, a prompt will also appear if you can interact with something.

4 NO PAIN, NO GAIN
Dying is OK, it's how you learn. You can find out how strong enemy attacks are or whether you'll survive a fall from a high point. You'll boss it in no time after that.

5 SOUNDS GREAT
Games can look pretty but sound is just as important. The music can change when there's danger and audio cues are key to knowing when an enemy is about to attack.

6 OFF THE BEATEN PATH
Very much the case in big open-world games but still possible in shorter, story-based adventures, developers always put in secrets. Take your time and look out for them!

So long city
Stardew Valley

3 It begins with your grandfather giving you a letter he tells you to open when you're older and "feel crushed by the burden of modern life." Years later, working in a soulless office, it's time to reach for that envelope. It turns out he left you his farm in Stardew Valley, so it's time to hop on the bus and start over.

Hello Cappy!
Super Mario Odyssey

4 Mario has to rescue Princess Peach, but Bowser manages to destroy his cap! New friend Cappy isn't just a replacement; he can be thrown to capture other creatures. After you've seen Mario take control of a frog, a Goomba, or even a T-Rex, you'll never think of *Mario* games the same way again.

Flower power
Undertale

5 *Undertale* is a very unusual indie RPG about a child who has fallen down a hole into the Underground. You first meet a flower called Flowey, who seems like a friendly character who will teach you the basics of the game. That's when you're hit by a nasty surprise . . .

> * Don't you have anything better to do?

Father and son, and geese
Golf Story

6 It looks like a retro RPG but instead you're playing golf. It's immediately charming when your dad takes you golfing. Besides serving as a basic golfing tutorial, it's also quality father-son bonding time, including the bad dad jokes.

> Focus on your shot, son.

Self-destruct sequence
Super Metroid

7 Bounty hunter Samus Aran thought it was "Mission Accomplished" after handing over the last surviving Metroid larva to scientists at Ceres Space Colony. But when a distress signal comes from the colony, it all begins again.

A new hope?
Final Fantasy XII: The Zodiac Age

8 There's a lot to take in: a royal wedding and war with an evil empire. A lot of people die. Hope comes in the form of a street orphan, a dashing rogue, his alien partner, and an exiled princess. Wait, were you thinking *Star Wars*?

Boy meets Colossus
Shadow of the Colossus

9 Your hero has already taken a long perilous journey to reach the Forbidden Land where he hopes to resurrect the girl he loves. To do this, you must slay the colossi who roam the land. And what fearsome, beautiful things they are!

Titan worlds Xenoblade Chronicles 2

10 As Rex, you live a simple life on the back of a titan called Gramps. But soon you'll discover whole countries that exist on the back of enormous titans. Once you meet Blades, living weapons that take the form of humans or beasts, you're just beginning to scratch the surface . . .

THE EXPERT SAYS . . .
CHRIS BELL
Game designer of Journey and What Remains of Edith Finch

Looking down, we discover our body: arm in a cast, bouquet and journal in our lap. Pulling away the flowers reveals a name, Edith Finch. We open the journal and she begins to speak:

"A lot of this isn't going to make sense, and I'm sorry about that. I'm just going to start at the beginning, with the house."

As illustrated by the opening of *What Remains of Edith Finch*, in mere moments we can establish a tone, place, and perspective, hint at what's come before or what lies ahead, introduce important characters, their relationships, and point to the big questions they seek answers to.

Let's not let a moment go to waste.

PINBALL FX3

EVERYTHING'S BETTER WITH FRIENDS

If you've ever been able to play on a physical **pinball machine, you know the joy they bring—the kinetic energy, the lights and sounds, the sounds of the flippers.** It's hard to have a full-size pinball machine in your home, but *Pinball FX3* more than makes up for that by offering a wide selection of amazing tables— including a bunch based on Marvel's characters!

Pinball FX3 isn't a pure simulation of pinball, it should be noted, instead throwing in extra mini-games and effects that just wouldn't be possible in a real-world table. But we say: "Why not?" It's boring to stick with what you can do in the real world, and being able to go that bit further when you're playing the Hulk, Captain America, or the Avengers' tables is always a great deal of fun.

STATS

3 TABLES IN THE ORIGINAL *PINBALL FX*

28,000 videos about *Pinball FX* on YouTube

9 ZEROES REQUIRED FOR THE SCORE 1,000,000,000 ACHIEVEMENT

1 BALL in the one-ball challenge, the purest pinball experience!

TOP 5 SCI-FI TABLES

The best of *Pinball FX3's* space-inspired tables

ALIENS PINBALL

1 The movie might be rated R, but the pinball table definitely isn't—and while it isn't as terrifying as the cinema version, Aliens Pinball does manage to bring the tension and panic in a way that's fun to hit balls around in. It's also got an amazing soundtrack.

EARTH DEFENSE

4 One of the *Pinball FX* classic tables, Earth Defense sees a 1950s B-movie style alien invasion with you, the pinball player, fighting it off. How? Well, by getting high scores of course! It's basic compared to later tables, but Earth Defense has a pureness that makes it a lot of fun still.

STAR WARS PINBALL: DARTH VADER

2 There are plenty of *Star Wars* tables offered in *Pinball FX3*, but we're going with Darth Vader just because he's the coolest bad guy in the history of . . . well, anything! Naturally he'd be able to cheat if he were playing pinball, what with the Force and all.

PORTAL PINBALL

3 One of the best gaming series ever made has a brilliant pinball table based on it. Not only is it great to play, full of extras and mini-games, it's also funny with GLaDOS's voice actor from the original games recording new lines.

WORLD WAR HULK

5 As with *Star Wars*, there are plenty of Marvel tie-in tables, but we're going with the lesser known World War Hulk thanks to the fact it's possible to achieve massive high scores on the table. You can even reach the billions!

TIPS & TRICKS

Pick your controls
There are a few different ways you can operate the left and right side flippers—find what works for you and stick with it.

Learn the table
Pinball is about learning the table and where you need to hit the ball. Stay on one table and just practice loads.

Multiply
Find out how to increase the bonus multiplier and hit it as much as possible to lead to *huge* points at the end of your turn.

Compete
Pinball FX3 is a superb game to play against friends, as you don't have to be playing at the same time. Try to beat everyone's scores!

Give a nudge
Nudging is cheating, and if you do it too much you will lose a ball automatically—but used carefully, a nudge can mean big points.

DID YOU KNOW?

The word "Lego" comes from the Danish phrase "leg godt" ("play well"). Even the name has been built . . . from words!

WON'T LEGO OF YOUR TIME

LEGO WORLDS

Whoever first had the idea of combining LEGO and video games was a genius, and few games feel like playing with real-world LEGO like this one. You're given an endless number of randomly generated little planets—literally worlds made out of LEGO—to play on and with. The more you explore and level up, the more you can do and build. Use your Discover tool to copy objects, vehicles, and characters; then buy them with studs, and place as many of them as you like!

Don't like the look of your current world? Change the ground you stand on by raising or lowering it, or plant trees and build a treehouse. Maybe pull out a jetpack, and use it to fly to the top of a castle . . . Your world, your rules.

STATS

100 Gold Bricks needed for Master Builder status

2 people can play together, online or offline

LEGO *Worlds* is available on **4 formats**

1 billion studs required for the Billionaire! Achievement or Trophy

NAVIGATING LEGO WORLDS

TOOLS AND TOYS

There are lots of gadgets for you to play around with. You're very quickly given the basics you need to shape the world around you and copy and paste objects you find, but there's more to it than that. This cool grappling hook, for example, will attach itself to *anything*.

THE MINI-MAP

As you walk around each unique world, your mini-map will help you find various things of interest. The blue arrow shows your position and the direction you're facing. Characters with tasks for you are marked with icons, and so are opportunities to win a Gold Brick. Go chase them down!

BE A PAL

There's a huge amount to unlock in LEGO *Worlds*, and a lot of it is given to you as rewards for helping characters out. If you see somebody with an exclamation point above their head, they have a job for you. See what they want, and what they can give.

YOUR ROCKET

How do you travel from one world to another? You rock a rocket, of course! Loading screens see you fly your ship through space, and you land it on each new world you discover. This is also how you level up; feed your rocket Gold Bricks for new explorer titles.

Jump (A)
Action (X)
Put Away (B)

TIPS & TRICKS

Go for gold
If you're having trouble finding Gold Bricks, just visit a new world. There's a never-ending supply of them, after all!

Building friendships
When a character asks you to finish a building, it doesn't have to look pretty for you to get a pretty reward …

Pesky skeletons
Night-time enemies giving you a hard time? Just pull out your Sky Spinner and make it day once again. Simple!

Sticky situations
If it looks like you're stuck, pause the game, and you can skydive back into your current world from there.

I like to move it
Something in your way? You can move and remove objects you've placed yourself … and also ones that were already there.

TOP 10 DUOS

Mario and Luigi

1 The most famous brothers in gaming take top-spot as the greatest duo. The pair have been jumping on Goombas and beating Bowser together for over 30 years. They've appeared solo in their own great games, but the two brothers are usually found in titles like *Super Mario 3D World* and *Mario & Luigi: Paper Jam*.

Trainer & Pokémon

2 Everyone remembers their first Pokémon. The Pokémon we pick at the beginning of any *Pokémon* game—Rowlet, Litten, or Popplio in *Pokémon Sun & Pokémon Moon*—is the only one that sticks by our side throughout the epic journey to become a Pokémon master. That creates a special bond between the cute little creature and ourselves as we watch it grow and become more powerful while exploring the world together.

Ryu and Ken

3 Most duos on this list work together, but Ryu and Ken are different. While the two have been known to back each other up from time to time, the source of their bond is their friendly rivalry. These *Street Fighter* legends have been doing battle with each other for years, always trying to prove to the other that they are the best.

Sonic and Tails

4 The kind nature of Tails makes him the perfect complement to the cocky hero Sonic. Tails first joined Sonic in *Sonic The Hedgehog 2* in 1992. You could play cooperatively, or race against each other. The twosome are still speeding side by side!

6 SIDEKICK SPINOFFS
The best games featuring members of iconic duos

LUIGI'S MANSION
Stepping out of Mario's shadow, Luigi is forced to face his fears in his series set in a haunted mansion. You must use Luigi's flashlight to stun ghosts and suck them up with the Poltergust 3000.

YOSHI'S WOOLLY WORLD
Yoshi started as a sidekick to Mario, but the loveable dinosaur became the star in *Super Mario World 2: Yoshi's Island*. Since then, Yoshi has had plenty of games, including *Yoshi's Woolly World*.

MARIO + RABBIDS: KINGDOM BATTLE
The Raving Rabbids first appeared in the *Rayman* series. Their popularity led to them getting their own game series.

CAPTAIN TOAD'S TREASURE TRACKER
Treasure Tracker is a fantastic puzzle game where you have to guide Captain Toad through many cool 3-D environments.

DIDDY KONG RACING
Back in the Nintendo 64 days, Donkey Kong's little buddy, Diddy Kong, got his own kart-racing title. Naturally, Donkey Kong appears as one of the racers.

SECRET AGENT CLANK
Clank is at his best when he's with Ratchet, but he still appeared in a game of his own. Along with the action from the main series, the game features a rhythm-action style stealth system.

Donkey Kong and Diddy Kong

5 A great duo works together. Donkey Kong and Diddy Kong do just that. In *Donkey Kong Country: Tropical Freeze*, Diddy Kong can ride on Donkey Kong's back and use his jetpack to help Donkey Kong hover. Diddy Kong can also hop off to collect bananas and jump on monsters!

Ratchet and Clank

6 The friendship between Ratchet and Clank has not only been the subject of a series of games, but a movie too. They have foiled the plans of alien invaders and saved the world together many times over, working together to bash, their way to victory.

THE EXPERT SAYS . . .
JAMES MARSDEN
Developer at Futurlab, creators of *Tiny Trax* and *Velocity 2X*

Ken and Ryu are my favorite gaming duo. They are such pure representations of male ego at two extremes. Pulling off my first purposeful dragon punch in the arcade was the single most influential gaming moment for me.

Professor Layton and Luke

7 Right at the core of the *Professor Layton* series' charm is the relationship between Professor Layton and Luke Triton. Professor Layton is a mentor figure for Luke to look up to, though there are times when the Professor needs Luke's help. A great puzzle-loving pair.

The Squid Sisters

8 The Squid Sisters, Marie and Callie, made their debuts in *Splatoon*. They announce events and updates and host Splatfest events. The two aren't on hosting duties in *Splatoon 2*, but the double act do return. Marie guides you through the single-player mode and Callie appears as a boss.

Yooka and Laylee

9 The adventure-loving chameleon Yooka and the wise-cracking bat Laylee are inseparable. The two each have their own special abilities that help them work together to explore the colorful cartoon platformer that is *Yooka-Laylee*. Yooka's tongue can be used to snap up objects and Laylee can stun enemies with her Sonar Shot, to give just a couple of examples.

Snip and Clip

10 *Snipperclips* is a game built on playing with a friend, cutting the duo Snip and Clip into shapes to complete levels. They don't say anything, but they are still full of personality thanks to the brilliant facial expressions they make!

HALO WARS 2

THE GREATEST SCI-FI SERIES EVER?

When the first *Halo* game launched for the original Xbox, it changed everything for first-person action games. The series broke records and has been going strong for over 17 years. Each game has introduced something new to freshen up the experience and the older games have been remastered for the Xbox One. The *Halo Wars* spin-offs changed the gameplay to real-time strategy. In *Halo Wars 2*—the series' most recent release—you control an entire army as you try to outsmart your opponent by building a base and gathering resources. It will test your ability to multitask, think ahead, and react to different combat situations.

STATS

MORE THAN 70 MILLION copies sold across all games

13 *Halo* games have been released **HALO**

6 billion hours have been played across all games on Xbox Live

7.4 million views for the E3 trailer on Xbox's channel

KNOW YOUR BASE

TURRETS

In the four corners of the base are spaces to construct watchtowers, siege turrets, or basic turrets. You can upgrade the basic turret to anti-air, anti-vehicle, or anti-infantry. Selecting the correct turret comes down to educated guessing, as the enemy will try to hide the different types of units that they have.

THE MINI MAP

When the battle starts, everything except your base will be covered in a dark grey fog. You must send units to explore these areas and uncover the map. Know which color you are and keep an eye out for any enemy colors popping up. Keep checking to look for any incoming attacks.

BUILDINGS

Depending on what you build, these allow you to generate power, build new units, research abilities for units, or be upgraded to build and research further. Knowing what structures to build first can be the difference between winning and losing.

SUPPLIES AND UNITS

Resources and power are required for creating and upgrading your units and buildings. Making sure you are gathering these and using them efficiently is key. Also in this menu is your unit limit. To start with, you can only have 80 units, but upgrading your base can increase this amount.

FurianReseigh86

51/80   247   355   2

ALSO CHECK OUT . . .

StarCraft II
Now a free-to-play game, *Starcraft* has three armies to choose from. If you prefer playing on your own against the AI, there's a number of expansions if the campaign leaves you really wanting more.

Destiny 2
Bungie, the original developer of *Halo*, left the series to create a new franchise, *Destiny*. You can explore the vast world alone or choose to team up with your buddies to complete the different quests or raid the dungeons.

GLOSSARY

4K
Ultra high-definition resolution, supported by high-end TVs and monitors. The actual resolution is 3840x2160, boasting four times as many pixels as a 1080p display.

AI
"Artificial intelligence," the code used to make in-game characters behave as they do. *The Last Guardian* is a great example of complex AI, used to make Trico behave like a real creature, but it's also what powers enemies in nearly every game.

AR
Augmented reality; a fusion of the real world and digital assets. *Pokémon GO* uses this to great effect by superimposing wild Pokémon over a live feed from your phone's camera, and various Vita and 3DS games also embrace this new technology.

Battle royale
A genre that combines last-one-standing gameplay with survival and exploration elements. Best demonstrated in *Fortnite: Battle Royale*.

Boss
A bigger, badder enemy commonly seen at the end of a level or guarding something particularly valuable. These larger foes tend to test all of your gaming skills and come with amazing rewards if you're able to beat them.

Bug
An error in a game that causes something unexpected to happen. May also be referred to as a glitch, depending on the nature of the bug. Some are extremely minor—such as several objects clipping into one another—while the most harmful can completely prevent progress. Save often, just in case!

Camping
The act of hanging around in one spot in a multiplayer game, usually either near where enemies spawn into a map or in a remote area, using a long-range weapon to repeatedly pick off players. Camping is usually frowned upon by rivals.

Casting
Can be short for either "broadcasting"—using services like Twitch, Beam, and YouTube to stream live gameplay—or "shoutcasting," which is play-by-play commentary of a gaming event, much like with live sports on TV.

BETA
A GAME IN AN UNFINISHED STATE, SOMETIMES WITH SELECT PLAYERS (A "CLOSED BETA") OR THE PUBLIC AT LARGE (AN "OPEN BETA") INVITED TO TEST KEY FEATURES AHEAD OF RELEASE. OCCASIONALLY, DEVELOPERS WILL OFFER THIS ACCESS EVEN EARLIER—THIS IS KNOWN AS THE "ALPHA" PHASE.

CCG

"Collectible card game," although you may also see TCG, which is "trading card game." They're effectively the same thing, though—games like *Hearthstone* where you earn new cards to make the very best deck you can.

Clutch

An unlikely comeback against all the odds is known as a clutch play. A good example would be using your Ultimate as the last hero standing to wipe out the enemy team, and prevent the payload from being delivered in the dying seconds of an *Overwatch* game.

Co-op

Teaming up with other players to work together toward a common goal. Co-op games usually increase the difficulty based on the number of players, so bear that in mind if you don't feel like your group is up to the challenge!

Cosplay

The art of creating costumes based on video-game characters, and often wearing them to events and conventions. Cosplay isn't limited to video games—enthusiasts also cosplay as movie, comic book, and anime characters as well!

Cross-up

An attack that forces the opponent to block from the opposite direction in a fighting game, usually performed by jumping over them to clip them in the back of the head. Some characters can perform cross-ups by dashing or teleporting through opponents as well.

DLC

Downloadable content. Extra levels, maps, characters, outfits, items, and modes made available for a game after release are collectively known as DLC.

DPS

"Damage per second," which can either refer to how much damage a character or weapon is able to do, or even characters whose role is primarily to deal damage, such as Black Mages in *Final Fantasy XIV*, or Tracer in *Overwatch*.

EASTER EGG

A SECRET HIDDEN IN A GAME THAT TYPICALLY SERVES NO FUNCTION OTHER THAN TO AMUSE OR ENTERTAIN. THESE CAN SOMETIMES BE REFERENCES TO OTHER GAMES, OR EVEN OTHER MEDIA ENTIRELY.

eSports

Professional gaming, as played by both individuals and full teams depending on the game being played. Prize pools are often massive for the biggest events, and the standard of play is incredibly high—major events are even broadcast live, just like a real sporting event.

F2P

"Free-To-Play," referring to games that can be downloaded and played for free. These often have some kind of in-game purchases, so watch out for those, but remember: never spend anything without getting your parents' permission!

FPS

First-person shooter—a game genre where you see through the eyes of the character, like *Destiny 2* or *Star Wars Battlefront II*.

Frame rate

The number of individual images that make up one second of moving game visuals. 30 frames per second (30fps) is common, and offers relatively smooth performance, with higher frame rates looking even smoother.

GG

"Good game." This is used in chat after multiplayer games in order to congratulate everyone involved on their success.

Griefing

Doing something just to annoy other players in a multiplayer game. This can be anything from standing in a doorway, so people can't get through, to attacking your own teammates. Don't do this—play nice!

Grinding

Repeating the same actions over and over again, like running in circles in tall grass in *Pokémon* to raise your team's levels, or doing the same quest repeatedly in *Monster Hunter* in the hopes of getting a rare reward.

HDR

A RELATIVELY NEW TERM, HDR STANDS FOR "HIGH DYNAMIC RANGE," AND IS SOMETHING YOU ONLY SEE IN NEW, HIGH-END DISPLAYS AND TVS. SUPPORTED GAMES BOAST MUCH BRIGHTER AND MORE VIBRANT COLORS IN HDR THAN ON A STANDARD SET—*REZ'S* AREA X IS ONE MIND-BLOWING EXAMPLE.

Indie

"Independent," refers to games or studios that don't have support from a major publisher. Indie studios are typically quite small, but the games that they create are often incredibly creative and original.

Kiting

The act of manipulating enemy placement to your advantage, such as a tank pulling a boss away from other players in an MMO, or Link running circles around enemies that only have close-range attacks.

Lag

A delay between player inputs and on-screen actions, usually caused by poor connections in online games. Minor lag is generally bearable, but extreme cases can make games unplayable.

Leaderboard

A high-score table. These are usually online elements, so you can see how your best results compare against the world's greatest players!

Metroidvania

A genre where exploration and back-tracking are key features, using new abilities that are unlocked to allow you to open previously inaccessible areas. *Ori and the Will of the Wisps* is one such example.

Mid-laner

A player who stays in the central area in MOBAs like *Dota 2*. There are also top and bottom-laners.

MMO

"Massively multiplayer online," games where many players can connect and communicate with one another. Most common are RPGs, but some—like *Sea of Thieves*—tackle other genres as well.

MOBA

"Multiplayer online battle arena" describes online games such as *League of Legends* and *Dota 2*. It's a relatively new genre, but one of the most popular in the world today!

Mod

Additional software that can alter how a game looks or plays, or even add completely new features. Though most common on PC, these are starting to be seen on consoles as well.

Noob

This is short for "newbie," a term used to describe someone who is new to playing a particular game. However, it is more commonly heard as an insult used against bad players.

NPC

NPC—or non-playable character—is the term used to refer to a non-hostile character. They might be important, like a quest-giver, or they might just be someone who exists in the game world.

PATCH

A POST-RELEASE UPDATE FOR A GAME THAT FIXES BUGS AND/OR ADDS NEW CONTENT. THESE ARE GROWING INCREASINGLY COMMON.

Permadeath

Refers to games where progress is lost upon death, forcing players to start over from scratch. Titles such as *Nuclear Throne* and *Don't Starve* are good examples of this.

Port

A game that is adapted from one system to another, sometimes with improvements (if the new system is more powerful than the original), or cuts to get it running on a weaker platform.

Post-game

Not all games end when the credits roll—in some cases, that's when the real fun begins! Games like *Pokémon* are rich in post-game content, and there's loads you can do after the game is "over."

PvE

"Player Versus Environment," a term used to refer to modes in games (typically ones with multiplayer components) where players take on AI opponents together rather than competing against one another.

PvP

The opposite of PvE, this means "Player Versus Player," meaning competitive multiplayer modes rather than co-operative ones.

Reboot

A game that looks to reinvent a series while returning to its roots, usually reverting to a basic title rather than using numbers or subtitles.

Remaster

This is a little different to a full remake—remasters tend to be slight upgrades of older games for new systems, using the same characters and levels, often sporting enhanced graphics or new modes.

Re-spec

Being able to cancel and redo things like skill-point distribution or other stats, enabling you to deal with various situations by quickly changing a character's specializations in a matter of seconds. A very useful feature!

Rogue-like

A genre of games where procedural generation is used to make every dungeon, session, or adventure different. It's named after classic 1980 dungeon-crawler *Rogue*.

RPG

"Role-playing game," sometimes encountered with additional letters: JRPG refers to Japanese titles, ARPG is used for action-heavy RPGs, MMORPG means online games, while SRPG means "strategy RPG," describing games such as *Fire Emblem*.

RTS

"Real-time strategy," a genre that shot to popularity with games like *Command & Conquer* and *StarCraft*, now dominated by the likes of the *Total War* series.

SANDBOX

OPEN-WORLD GAMES WHERE PLAYERS ARE FREE TO PLAY AROUND AND EXPERIMENT HOWEVER THEY WISH— THINGS LIKE THE HUB AREAS IN LEGO GAMES, OR THE OPEN WORLDS OF *MINECRAFT* AND *DRAGON QUEST BUILDERS*.

Scrub

An insult aimed at bad players, or those who rely on cheap, basic tactics, such as spamming the same moves over and over in a fighting game.

Sherpa

A player who helps others through difficult content in multiplayer games, such as Raids in *Destiny 2*. Sherpas are usually experts who know their way around, and often there's little in it for them outside of just being helpful.

Season Pass

Modern games often have downloadable extras that offer the ability to pre-purchase all of it in one bundle—this kind of package is known as a season pass, but actual contents will vary from game to game.

Speedrun

The act of playing through games as quickly as possible, often using glitches and other tricks to beat games in record time. Runners often post their best efforts online, and compete with others on ranking sites to see who is the fastest at any given game.

Tank

A strong character in a game whose job is to soak up damage, and protect more fragile characters. Tanks are common in MMO games, but you'll also find them in class-based online games like *Overwatch*.

Maker stages, and *Roblox* games are all perfect examples of this.

Vanilla

Used to refer to the original version of a game before patches and updates are applied. Vanilla base games are sometimes still supported (as is the case with *Destiny 2*), but in other cases, the only way to play the original versions is on special fan-run servers.

VR

Virtual reality, the hot new technology that is taking the gaming world by storm. Players wear headsets and are completely immersed in the action, moving as if it's really happening around them.

Whiff

To miss with an attack or move. This can either be completely accidental or done intentionally to mess with other players, or for some other purpose, like building meter in fighting games.

Top-deck

In a card game, top-decking is where you find yourself relying on the next card you draw, whether it's because your hand is empty or because you find yourself in a situation where there are only a couple of cards in your deck that will actually be useful.

Trolling

Misbehaving in an online game purely to annoy other players. This comes in many forms, from getting in the way of others, or hurting your own team, to intentionally doing the opposite of what you're supposed to do. Don't do it!

UGC

"User-generated content," describes things that players have made using in-game tools. Original *Minecraft* worlds, *Super Mario*

XP

"EXPERIENCE POINTS," USED TO LEVEL UP IN RPGS OR ANY PROGRESS SYSTEM LIKE THOSE OF THE *FORZA* GAMES. SOMETIMES WRITTEN AS EXP, BUT THE PURPOSE IS TYPICALLY THE SAME— GAIN LOADS AND LEVEL UP!